GOD MADE VISIBLE

GOD MADE VISIBLE

SEEING HIS GLORY
EXPERIENCING HIS PRESENCE

STEVE C. SHANK

WHAT OTHERS ARE SAYING

It is rare to use words such as "searching" and "probing" to describe a book. But in this case, it's true! I did not read Pastor Steve C. Shank's new book; it read me! I started out to read the manuscript of a friend; I finished on my knees before the Lord. Steve weaves his own encounters with the glory of God together with the biblical revelation in a way that is both illuminating and inspiring.

Dr. Gary Kellner
International Coalition for Christian Leadership
www.iccleadership.com

God Made Visible is an invitation past the barriers of the flesh, through the path of Christ's nature, and into the greater glory of God! Steve's own journey, the testimonies of his friends, and the wisdom of his mentor, Arthur Burt, as well as Steve's thorough teaching all take us beyond the shallow or fleeting descriptions we often ascribe to the word

*'glory' and into greater depths of understanding, ready for
personal experience!*

Joey LeTourneau, Author
Heavenly Hope Ministries
Blog: joeyletourneau.com

*Reading Pastor Steve C. Shank's book, God Made Visible,
was a true inspiration. I was humbled, convicted, and
thoroughly blessed by what I read. A warning to the reader:
If you are not genuinely serious about your relationship
with God and His glory, do not read this book! It is for
those who genuinely want to pursue God and everything
He has for us as believers. If you are the kind of believer
who wants a truly intimate and powerful relationship with
God and His glory, you need to read this book. It will
change your walk with Him.*

Dr. Denny Nissley
Executive Director
www.christinaction.com

*Many Church leaders over the centuries have asked the
question, "What must we do in order to see God's power
and wonders?" The Church has analyzed historical moves of
God, created formulas, gone through the motions, and used
trial and error; but most of it has just fallen flat. You'll
find out in this book that maybe we've just been asking the
wrong question. The answer is not in "what" we do, nearly
as much as in "why" we do it. In this important book,*

Steve C. Shank draws the connection between humility and "Revival." He helps us avoid the pitfalls of pride, and stay on the path of humility—ensuring that God gets all the glory! This book is PACKED with time-proven wisdom from one of Steve's mentors, as proven out in his own life. Don't miss it!

Joshua Greeson
Author of God's Will Is Always Healing:
Crushing Theological Barriers to Healing
www.facebook.com/GodsWillisAlwaysHealing

Steve C. Shank allows us to see into his special relationship with a father of the Church, revealing many of the truths that Arthur Burt has shared with him over the years. These truths have molded Steve and helped to make him the man of God that he is today. The journey detailed in this book grips you and makes you want to read on. Steve lays out the scriptural basis for the glory of God and includes many examples of how God is still at work revealing His glory—a true must read.

Jim Rogers, International Revivalist
www.experiencinghispresence.org

Why do we do the things we do for God? Is it for the glory of man or the glory of God? Is it because we want to please man or please God? Are we living for the audience of One or for a different audience? This book deals with these questions. I love the way Steve cuts to the chase, showing how many leaders were not able to handle the glory of God once it began to manifest in their lives on a regular basis. Will you be one of those who are able to handle the glory of God in these last days and finish your course well? Humility is key! Let this book help you develop a hunger for humility and for the glory of God to manifest in your life!

Mark R. Anderson
Evangelist and Author of
Humility: The Hidden Key to Walking in
Signs and Wonders
www.markandersonministries.com

Pastor Steve C. Shank came to Mexico with us in 2013, and we could literally sense a strong manifestation of God's glory coming to the churches as the sick were healed and lives transformed. I believe that the anointed message in his new book will enable us to be "glory carriers" and accelerate God's purpose, power, and anointing in our lives and ministries. It's a new day and a new season of His greater glory!

Pastor Aaron Kolb
Missionary/Church Planter
World Changers, Inc., P.O. Box 439, Oak Grove,
Missouri 64075

DEDICATION

To those who have helped to make us all that we are in life—parents, spouses, pastors, teachers, authors, coaches, and, yes, even little children—we are forever grateful to you all!

A TRIBUTE TO ARTHUR W. BURT

Our belief system is made up of a set of deeply held convictions that we have accumulated over the years. Every person's life is governed by what he or she believes, whether it's the three-year-old toddler just getting started or the 103-year-old saint just finishing the race. In our belief system there can be a mixture of proven facts, infallible truths, superstitions, deceptions, and fables. That being the case, whom have you allowed into your life as your mentors?

Mentors? Yes, mentors! We gain a tremendous advantage when we connect with wise and trusted teachers/counselors; in another word, mentors. As I look back over my own 60 years on planet earth, I can see that five mentors have been instrumental in helping me become the person I am today. Three of them were my grandparents' age. Although I never met them personally but only through books, I feel like I know them in spirit—the way they think and how they conducted themselves in various situations. After reading thousands of pages of their writings, I was able to glean the gold from their teachings and incorporate it into my own life. The fourth mentor taught me nearly every day for a year and then in a continual way through his own books and recordings until he finished his race. What an immense blessing of wealth we have available to us through sound and tested books. A person's wisdom and ministry can live on and continue to help and impact generations to come! Then, of course, we have the Book of all books—the Bible. Through it we get to know the greatest Teacher and Mentor who has ever lived—Jesus. Although we have not met Him in the flesh, we have met Him in the spirit as we have feasted upon the life-giving words of His Holy Book.

This brings me to the reason I'm writing this book: my fifth mentor, Brother Arthur, or "Uncle Arthur" as he is lovingly called by many. Arthur W. Burt was born May 12, 1912, at Whitley Bay on the northeast coast of England. He attended his first Gospel meetings in 1926, conducted by evangelist Stephen Jeffries. Victoria Hall was filled three times a day with 6,000 people in each meeting. Many were brought to the meetings in ambulances and were instantly healed by the power of God. Arthur witnessed a young lady who was born blind receive her sight, and then he knew that Jesus was real! As a result, he was born again on May 1, 1927, at nearly fifteen years of age.

At age eighteen Arthur left home to preach the Gospel. He traveled by horse and buggy and drove some of the first automobiles. When he was 22 years old, he met British evangelist Smith Wigglesworth. Arthur lived with Smith for a season, carried his bags, and even slept in the same bedroom with him. In 1958 while Arthur was pastoring a church in England, the Spirit of the Lord spoke and told him to leave the pastorate and "walk the land." He has since gone to over 44 nations, and I heard him say 25 years ago that he quit counting his trips to the USA after 200.

Arthur's life and ministry are marked by transparency—he has no desire to please people, only God. You will often hear him say that motives are all-important: It's not what you do that matters; it's why you do it. All that counts is what is done by God's Spirit—no fleshly gimmicks. Arthur frequently will expose himself by sharing his worst misdeeds and biggest failures with the hope that you will learn from his mistakes and be spared from doing the same things. Anyone who has heard him minister will tell you that he is a storyteller extraordinaire. He has the God-given ability to paint pictures with words in parable style, depositing gold nuggets for all to ponder. After a pearl of wisdom is imparted, he will often say, "Selah—pause, and think of that."

Arthur Burt has been a teacher, preacher, and prophetic voice to the Body of Christ all over the world. For over 50 years, his message has been that the last move of God on the earth will be a ministry of His Presence, and that He's preparing a people who can handle the

Presence of God to the glory of God! Like a trumpet, Arthur Burt has sounded forth this message wherever the wind of the Spirit has blown him.

DEAR BROTHER ARTHUR

At the time of this writing, you are 101 years old, my dear friend. You have gone around the world so many times, you have lost count. You've been to so many places, seen so many things, and learned so much in the process. I want to thank you from the bottom of my heart, and I give you my honor, esteem, and gratitude for taking the time and effort to minister into my life. I will forever appreciate you and the impact you have made upon me. Much heartfelt love to you, Brother Arthur!—Steve C. Shank

Photo Courtesy of Pierre Tullier

SPECIAL THANKS TO

Linda Holbrook, for your contribution of time, typing, and help with proofing the manuscript. I don't know many besides me who have been blessed by such a faithful secretary for nearly thirty-three years.

Martha Robbins, for your expert editing and for coming up with an excellent title for the book. Thank you, my friend.

Micah Hayden, for helping set up the arrangements for the publishing and cover design details. You're an excellent writer yourself, my daughter.

Steve Burt, for taking time to proofread the manuscript to ensure my quotes and representations of your father were accurate. I highly appreciate and esteem you and the fellowship at Bron Wendon, North Wales.

CONTENTS

Introduction xx

Chapter 1: Show Us Your Glory! 1

Chapter 2: The Glory of God?. 5

Chapter 3: Yours Is the Glory Forever! 21

Chapter 4: How Have the Mighty Fallen? 41

Chapter 5: Catching the Spider. 47

Chapter 6: The Domino Club 75

Chapter 7: To Judge or Not to Judge. 99

Chapter 8: A Beautiful Heart. 121

Chapter 9: Originations Are All Important. 141

Chapter 10: Demonstrations 151

Chapter 11: Now Is the Time 175

Endnotes 179

About the Author 182

INTRODUCTION

One of the main ministries of the Holy Spirit is to guide us into "all Truth" (John 16:13). Since "all Truth" is the goal, and none of us have arrived at the finish line yet, we will all be at different places in our spiritual walk. Consider that our gracious Father God wants to unveil and bring us into "all Truth." How vast and deep must be the ocean of God's knowledge! The Apostle Paul was given enough Truth to write fourteen books of the Bible, and yet he said of himself and his generation, "Now we see in a mirror, dimly" (1 Corinthians 13:12).

That being said, it's amazing how we subconsciously think that we are currently in possession of "all Truth." We very often will judge and reject a new revelation just because we've never heard it before. If we can't fit it into our current spiritual mindset, we reason and assume that it can't be true—we would've seen it already! As a young believer, I made the common mistake of rejecting any Truth that my church had not seen or sanctioned. The false assumption was that "all Truth" began and ended with "*my* church!" If we're all moving forward along the path to "all Truth," we should not be surprised or threatened to discover that no two people share the exact same views. Obviously there are things you have seen that I haven't, and vice versa. We can joyfully learn from each other and, therefore, help one another move forward.

Brother Arthur Burt and I have had many, many times when we sat together for hours and discussed the wonderful things of God. I sincerely believe that he is the wisest man that I have ever met, but there are a few things we don't see eye to eye on. Instead of letting those things separate us, our love, respect, appreciation, and friendship for one another has only grown deeper with time.

So my purpose for writing this book has been to fill it with as many gold nuggets for your life as possible. I will share insights and come from some angles that may be new to you. I know that our ears test words, just as our mouths taste food (Job 12:11). So test what is written here with the Bible and the witness of the Holy Spirit in your own heart. Take what you can use, incorporate it into your life, and pass it on to others! What you're not sure about, simply put it on the shelf. My desire is that your life will shine brighter and brighter to the glory of our Great Father God!

In addition to those at the start of each chapter, I will be giving you many quotes from Arthur Burt, each italicized, indented, and followed by the initials AB.

CHAPTER 1
SHOW US YOUR GLORY!

I had met God. I yearned and longed for His Presence. I just couldn't settle for anything less than living in God's Presence.

–Arthur Burt

"PLEASE, SHOW ME Your glory!" From the bottom of Moses' heart, he uttered forth his deepest desire to God (Exodus 33:18). Here was a man whose whole life had been marked by the supernatural. Think about his life with God. God had personally spoken to him from a burning bush and called him forth into ministry. Later God would speak to Moses face to face as a man speaks to his friend. It's safe to say that Moses knew God and His Presence better than anyone of his generation. He knew the ways of God and the promises of God, and he received much counsel and revelation from his many meetings with God. The first five books of the Bible came through Moses, so we know he was a man of the Word. He was a man of faith who is mentioned in that great faith chapter of Hebrews 11. Many, many times, he moved in faith with God, and God confirmed His Word with mighty signs and wonders!

Moses had seen the awesome power and authority of God on display. Over and over, he witnessed the incredible manifestations of God released in signs and wonders in order to deliver Israel from Egyptian bondage; and, of course, as he extended his rod of authority, the Red Sea was split open to make a way of escape. He saw and knew God's healing power: "There was none feeble among His tribes" (Psalm 105:37). Provision? Miraculously, God made food appear every day without fail for 40 years! How much would it take every day to feed a country of around three million people?

I believe Moses was the most outstanding, most often quoted figure of the Old Covenant; and yet, after all he had seen, known, and experienced with his God, this is the one thing he longed for more than anything else: "Please, show me Your glory!" If there's one thing we can conclude from Moses' life on earth with God, it's this: The more of God you come to know and experience, the more of God you want to know and experience! He is definitely the God of much more.

In Chapter 2 we will get a much better understanding of what God's glory is; but for now, let's say that God's glory is the sum total of all that God is, made visible for you to see and know.

I WANT TO SEE YOUR POWER AND YOUR GLORY!

Most of us are aware of the fact that God raised up David to be king and called him "a man after My own heart" (Acts 13:22). David loved the Presence of God and spent much time worshiping Him alone and also in the temple with others. But notice that with David, just as with Moses, his greatest desire was always pointing toward the glory of God! "So I have looked for You in the sanctuary, to see Your power and Your glory" (Psalm 63:2). David walked with God and knew God. He loved God and was satisfied with God. He had all kinds of experiences with God and, yet, he was always wanting to see Him, know Him, enjoy Him, and experience Him even more—and there's nothing wrong with that! God wants to be wanted. He wants us to know and experience Him in ever-increasing ways! David invites us to "taste and see" (Psalm 34:8). God is to be known, experienced, and enjoyed with your whole will, heart, mind, emotions, feelings—yes, your whole spirit, soul, and body. Jesus told us that eternal life, the God-kind of life, was to really get to know and experience the Father, the True and Living God; and likewise, to know, experience, and understand Jesus Christ Whom He sent (see John 17:3).

King David may be the most beloved character of the Old Covenant, a skilled musician and anointed worshiper of God. He will forever be known as "the man after God's own heart." So what is David's heart centered on when he makes his last recorded prayer in the Book of Psalms? "Blessed be His glorious name forever! And let the whole earth be filled with His glory. Amen and amen" (Psalm 72:19).

IS THIS FOR US TODAY?

We can clearly see that the two most outstanding people of the Old Covenant, Moses and David, shared the same burning passion to see and experience the glory of God. One of the main purposes of this book is to answer the question, "Is this something that all the rest of us can see, know, and experience today?" Does God desire for us to see and experience His glory? And if He does, what exactly *is* the "glory of God"?

CHAPTER 2
THE GLORY OF GOD?

Coming to the Church is a
demonstration of the Presence.

–Arthur Burt

WHEN WE TALK about the "glory of God," what exactly are we talking about? The Bible gives us simple definitions: heavy, weighty, outshining, effulgence, emanation, exhibition, excellence, greatness, inherent beauty. I like to say that it's what's inherently in God made manifest, or made visible; or, His glorious manifest Presence. It really helps us understand what the glory of God is like when we look at some of the recorded appearances of it in the Bible.

THE GOD OF GLORY

Notice that Stephen called our Father "the God of glory" (Acts 7:2) and actually saw the glory of God as he was being martyred: "But he, being full of the Holy Spirit, gazed into heaven and saw the glory of God" (Acts 7:55). When Isaiah looked into heaven at the throne of God, he said, "The house was filled with smoke" (Isaiah 6:4). Notice how Ezekiel describes the appearance of the glory of God: "Like the appearance of a rainbow in a cloud on a rainy day, so was the appearance of the brightness all around it. This was the appearance of the likeness of the glory of the Lord" (Ezekiel 1:28). Ezekiel shows us that the glory of the Lord can move, pause, and settle down over areas. "Then the glory of the Lord went up from the cherub, and paused over the threshold of the temple; and the house was filled with the cloud, and the court was full of the brightness of the Lord's glory" (Ezekiel 10:4).

COMING FROM HEAVEN TO EARTH

The glory of God does not just fill God's heavenly temple and surround His throne. It can also move and manifest upon the earth. "And behold, the glory of the God of Israel came from the way of the east. His voice was like the sound of many waters; and the earth shone with His glory.... And the glory of the Lord came into the temple by way of the gate which faces toward the east ... and behold, the glory of the Lord filled the temple" (Ezekiel 43:2, 4-5). We all remember how the shepherds were out in the fields watching over their flocks at night when an angel appeared to them and announced the birth of Jesus the Savior. "An angel of the Lord stood before them, and the glory of the Lord shone around them" (Luke 2:9).

And we can easily see how it was the glory of the Lord that was manifested at the dramatic conversion of Paul. "Suddenly a great light from heaven shone around me. And I fell to the ground and heard a voice.... Those who were with me indeed saw the light.... I could not see for the glory of that light" (Acts 22:6, 7, 9, 11).

Often the glory of God has manifested during wholehearted times of praise and worship. "When they lifted up their voice with ... instruments of music, and praised the Lord, saying: 'For He is good, for His mercy endures forever,' that the house, the house of the Lord, was filled with a cloud, so that the priests could not continue ministering because of the cloud; for the glory of the Lord filled the house of God" (2 Chronicles 5:13-14).

Notice, too, how the glory of the Lord did not accompany just the birth of Jesus but also manifested on and around Him during His earthly ministry. "And as He prayed, the appearance of His face was altered, and His robe became white and glistening.... Peter and those with him ... saw His glory.... A cloud came and overshadowed them.... And a voice came out of the cloud, saying, 'This is My beloved Son. Hear Him!'" (Luke 9:29, 32, 34, 35). Here we clearly see how the glory of God can come upon an individual and alter the appearance of his or her face. It can appear upon a person's clothing and cause it to become dazzling white, flashing with the brilliancy of lightning! After Moses' experience with the glory of the Lord, the skin of his face shone (Exodus 34:30).

GOD'S GLORY IS ACCOMPANIED BY HIS POWER

When John saw into God's heavenly temple, he said, "The temple was filled with smoke from the glory of God and from His power" (Revelation 15:8). Tremendous power was released when Jesus was raised from the dead, and the Bible says, "Christ was raised from the dead by the glory of the Father" (Romans 6:4). What a mighty release of God's power and glory burst forth on that glorious resurrection morning! Anyone who witnessed that explosive display of God's glory would have been forever affected! "And behold, there was a great earthquake; for an angel of the Lord descended from heaven, and came and rolled back the stone from the door, and sat on it. His countenance was like lightning, and his clothing as white as snow. And the guards shook for fear of him, and became like dead men" (Matthew 28:2-4).

As we have seen, the Bible associates these things with the glory of God: smoke, a cloud, multicolored hues like a rainbow in a cloud, a bright light. The glory of the Lord can move, fill up a house, appear outside of houses of worship, and alter a person's appearance, causing his or her face and clothing to shine; and God's glory carries such power that it can raise the dead and shake the earth!

MODERN DAY OCCURRENCES

I often ask people, "Do you believe God can do anything?" Usually they will answer, "Of course. He's God!" To which I will always wholeheartedly agree. Then I will proceed to tell them some of the miraculous things my friends and I have seen God do, and they say, "I don't believe that." This puts them into the category of an unbelieving believer, which of course is an oxymoron—a self-contradiction. Jesus Christ is the same today as He was yesterday (Hebrews 13:8). Who He was and what He did in Bible days is still Who He is and what He does today. Our Father God is forever the same and never changes (Malachi 3:6). The Holy Ghost acts the same today as He did in the Book of Acts.

I went to Bible College back in 1978, and one of my teachers had many experiences with the glory of God in the 1900s. Here are a few of the testimonies he shared with us; keep this in mind—they all happened in the USA.

One time as he was preaching, he saw seven-foot waves of bright, white clouds rolling in from the back of the auditorium. They eventually enveloped all the people and covered the preacher and the pulpit as well. The glory remained on the people for about fifteen minutes and then reversed itself and rolled back out as it had come. The result? Every unsaved or backslidden person had come forward and gotten right with the Lord!

Another time as he was preaching, a giant flash of light—brighter than 10,000 flashbulbs—went off and momentarily blinded everyone present. When they could see again, the altar was filled with lost people. Some had no knowledge of going to the front. They all made Jesus their Lord and were born again.

On another occasion, a mighty wind blew through the auditorium. Everyone present heard and felt it. A lady who was sick and at the point of death had been brought into the meeting on a stretcher. She instantly jumped up and ran around the auditorium, completely healed! Everyone there was saved, healed, and filled with the Holy Spirit.

In another service, a young adult man ran in off the street right at altar call time. He looked around wild-eyed, and it appeared as if his hair was standing on end. He told the preacher, "I am not a Christian, and I don't go to church; but I was walking down the street two blocks from here when a ball of fire came out of the air and hung three feet over my head. I followed it down the street, and it came in here. I want to be saved!"

"So I have looked for You in the sanctuary, to see Your power and Your glory" (Psalm 63:2).

A RELATIONSHIP WITH A PERSON OR A BOOK?

One of my callings is that of a Bible teacher. I absolutely love the Word of God! I exalt it as final authority and the solid foundation for everything that pertains to God and spirituality. But I am concerned that people have forgotten, or never knew, that the Bible is not an end in itself, but a means to bring people into a living encounter and personal relationship with God Himself. The purpose of the written Word is to lead you into a vital experience with the Living Word, Jesus Christ—not to make you an egghead, intellectual Christian; not just to fill your head with book knowledge. God is a Living God Who's to be known, worshiped, and adored. He's not a doctrine. When people *know* a lot of the Word, but don't *experience* a lot of the Word, they have a tendency to take on a Pharisee type of attitude. "Oh, you're so experience oriented," they say. "You need to love God with all your mind and be sound in doctrine!" Well, I agree with that, but don't you agree that God wants all that we see in the Word to be brought into manifestation to the glory and fame of His great Name, and so that others can see and know Him, too? God desires a people who are hungry for Him, who are eager to experience spiritual realities with Him, and who are not content merely with correct interpretations or sound doctrine.

YOU ARE THE MIRACLE OFFSPRING OF A MIRACLE GOD

Even though God is a spiritual, supernatural being, He can be known, experienced, and enjoyed just as any person can. Just as He has built physical capabilities into you so that you can know people on a physical level, He has built spiritual capabilities into you so that you can know and enjoy Him on a spiritual level.

The whole Bible is full of miraculous encounters that people had with the Living God. God wants to be known, and so He supernaturally makes Himself known. It's hard for me to fathom how people study the Bible and arrive at a miracle-free theology. Could it be because their current Christianity is lacking a living, conscious, experiencing of God?

ENCOUNTERS WITH GOD HIMSELF

Like a broken record, it's repeated over and over in scripture how the people of God had real experiences with God. Let's refuse to be satisfied with a run-of-the-mill book knowledge of the Lord—let's really get to know Him as well as we can!

Abram "The Lord appeared to Abram and said to him ..." (Genesis 17:1).

Jacob "I have seen God face to face" (Genesis 32:30).

Samuel "Now the Lord came and stood and called as at other times, 'Samuel! Samuel!'" (1 Samuel 3:10).

Elijah Experienced God by fire and by His "still small voice" (1 Kings 18:38 and 1 Kings 19:12-13).

Job "I have heard of You by the hearing of the ear, but now my eye sees You" (Job 42:5).

Isaiah "My eyes have seen the King, the Lord of hosts" (Isaiah 6:5).

Ezekiel "The heavens were opened and I saw visions of God" (Ezekiel 1:1).

Peter "And a voice came to him, 'Rise, Peter'" (Acts 10:13).

Disciples "Then their eyes were opened and they knew Him.... And they said to one another, 'Did not our heart burn within us while He talked with us?'" (Luke 24:31-32).

Paul "Then he fell to the ground, and heard a voice saying to him, 'Saul, Saul, why are you persecuting Me?'" (Acts 9:4).

John "I turned to see the voice that spoke with me. And having turned I saw ... One like the Son of Man" (Revelation 1:12-13).

GOD HAS PURPOSED THIS FOR YOU FROM THE BEGINNING

God said in the beginning, "Let Us make man in Our image, according to Our likeness" (Genesis 1:26). The first son and daughter of God walked in His Presence continually, with the capacity to know Him and relate to Him on His level. Our purpose on earth is no different—to be conformed to His image and walk in His Presence.

After Moses experienced the glory of God, his face shone with that glory. But instead of it increasing upon his life, it decreased. The degree of glory that God desires for our lives today exceeds that of Moses in quality, intensity, and longevity! God desires that we all reflect the Lord's glory with ever-increasing degrees of it; not a diminishment, but an increase. I am convinced that He desires His glory in every house of God, His glory in your home, His glory in your workplace, and His glory in your city! "But we all, with unveiled face, beholding as in a mirror the glory of the Lord, are being transformed into the same image from glory to glory, just as by the Spirit of the Lord" (2 Corinthians 3:18).

You see, it's God's desire to transform us all from

glory to glory into the image of the Lord. That word *transformed* means to be changed from the inside out, just as in its cocoon a caterpillar changes into a butterfly. God desires to change us from the inside out so that Christ in us comes fully forth and our lives glorify Him and are covered with His glory. Christ in you is the confident expectation you have of entering into His glory (see Colossians 1:27). As we regularly behold the glory of the Lord, look into His face, look into His Word, and soak in His Presence, we are being changed into His image by the mighty workings of the Spirit of the Lord.

EVERYONE SPEAKS OF HIS GLORY

Psalm 29:9 tells us of a time when everyone in God's temple spoke of His glory. The time is coming soon when whole churches will gather together with their hearts, minds, and voices centered upon His glory. Their longing desire will be to seek His Presence continually. (See 1 Chronicles 16:11.) We will all come to exalt the "King of glory" (Psalm 24:7); to express our love and adoration to the "Father of glory" (Ephesians 1:17); and to bow with humble hearts before the "Lord of glory" (1 Corinthians 2:8).

I love the heart's desire of this song, "Show Me Your Glory," by Jesus Culture.[1]

> I see the cloud, I step in
> I want to see Your glory as Moses did
> Flashes of light, and rolls of thunder
> I'm not afraid, I'm not afraid
>
> Show me Your glory, show me Your glory …
>
> I'm awed by Your beauty, lost in Your eyes
> I want to walk in Your presence like Jesus did
> Your glory surrounds me and I'm overwhelmed
> I'm not afraid, I'm not afraid
>
> Show me Your glory, show me Your glory …
>
> I long to look on the face of the One that I love
> Long to stay in Your presence, it's where I belong.

THE GREATER INCLUDES THE LESSER

Arthur Burt says this has been one of the greatest lessons he's learned in life: The greater includes the lesser. The lesser does not include the greater—it's the other way around.

Jesus demonstrated this in His teachings. He instructs us to seek first the Kingdom of God (the greater), then earthly provision (the lesser) God will supply. This is the order of God. The greater includes the lesser; but if I reverse the order and seek the lesser first, the lesser does not include the greater. **(AB)**

You will always see greater results when you're not after results first, but you're after God and His glory first. The greater (living in His Presence) far exceeds but includes the lesser (signs and wonders). Living in the Presence manifests an enabling power that more will be accomplished — including signs and wonders that follow after. It is my daily choice to know Him more intimately, instead of just seeking His acts. **(AB)**

When the King of kings is given His rightful throne in the castle of a man's heart, His residence there is an evident Presence in that man's life. The Giver of all gifts can manifest at any time through the vessel He is happy to reside in — in evangelism, prayer, intercession, discernment, prophecy, love, faith, joy, peace, healing, etc. His Presence is all inclusive. But if I focus on the gifts (the lesser) instead of the Lord Jesus (the greater), the order is wrong. **(AB)**

Signs serve a purpose in the Kingdom of God, but the sign is not the Treasure that you're after. I remember the first time I went to the massive department store Harrods in London. The building is a block long with three or four floors. It is full of signs made in the shape of a hand with a finger pointing you in the right direction—to coats, furniture, shoes, books, jewelry, etc. If I want to buy my wife a piece of gold jewelry, the sign that says *jewelry* is very helpful in leading me to my destination, but the sign is not the gold that I'm seeking! Treasure Jesus and steward His Presence as your highest desire and top priority. Jesus is the Gold! Signs always point to Him, and their purpose is to help people find their reason for being and their true fulfillment in Him.

MAY OUR DESIRE DEEPEN

Being a carrier of His Presence draws people to Jesus effectively. His Presence is attractive. Out of His Presence will manifest His person to draw mankind to Himself and an intimate relationship with Him. **(AB)**

There's such an attractiveness and vastness in God that no matter how much of Him we've seen and experienced, we want to see and experience Him more and more! My prayer for you as you read this book is that it will spark in you a deep desire to know the God of glory and to walk in and enjoy His Presence in ever-increasing ways: *Lord, we want to know and experience the heights and depths of You as we are conformed to the glorious image of Your Son.*

CHAPTER 3
YOURS IS THE GLORY FOREVER!

*We have a responsibility in stewardship to
learn to handle our gifts to God's glory.*

–Arthur Burt

A S WE HAVE just seen, one way God's glory is
described is this—what's inherently in God made
manifest, or His glorious manifest Presence.

We are well aware of these facts: When we make Jesus
our Lord and receive Him as our Savior, God dwells
in us and we become His temple. We are complete in
Him and become partakers of His divine nature; and
when we meet together, He is in our midst. Where can
we go from His Spirit? He will never leave us nor for-
sake us. He's in us and all around us, all the time! See
2 Corinthians 6:16; Colossians 2:10; 2 Peter 1:4; Matthew
18:20; Psalm 139:7; and Hebrews 13:5.

FROM THE INSIDE TO THE OUTSIDE

For instance, in our individual lives we want the Christ
who fills our interior to come forth and be seen on our

exterior. What good are His love, joy, peace, patience, power, and authority if they stay hidden within us? We are called to be demonstrations of who Christ is—we want Jesus on the inside of us to be seen on the outside!

By the same token, the unseen God can manifest with demonstrations of His Spirit in this physical world we live in. That's what we mean by the "manifest" Presence of God. That's called the glory! If you think about it, the only thing that sets us apart from the rest of the world is the Presence of God *revealed* in our midst. Without the King manifesting Himself in His kingdom, we look like just another dead religious system to the world. So every day my heart continues to say, "Show us Your glory!"

A SECOND MAJOR USE OF THE WORD GLORY

"Glory to God in the highest!" "We give You all the glory!" "For Thine is the kingdom, the power, and the glory forever, amen!"

When we say, "Glory be to God," what exactly do we mean? We mean that all the honor and fame should go to His great Name for Who He is and what He does in our midst. When God does a work in us individually or corporately, He should receive the credit, or glory, for what He's done. We should magnify Him with praise—glorify and boast in Him alone!

Notice how this is made clear in the scriptures I cite below:

- "Give unto the Lord the glory due to His name; worship the Lord in the beauty of holiness" (Psalm 29:2). We ascribe to the Lord the glory/honor/credit that He is due—He is worthy!

- "Not unto us, O Lord, not unto us, but to Your name give glory, because of Your mercy, because of Your truth" (Psalm 115:1). Where would we be without His mercy and truth? So the glory never goes to us but always to Him and Him alone.

- "I am the Lord, that is My name; and My glory I will not give to another, nor My praise to carved images" (Isaiah 42:8). Notice here that He calls it "His" glory. The honor/credit/glory that is His will never be given to men or angels, but especially not to idols! We are talking about the glory due Him for Who He is and for all that He does for us by His grace.

- "For who makes you differ from another? And what do you have that you did not receive? Now if you did indeed receive it, why do you glory as if you had not received it?" (1 Corinthians 4:7). What do we have that we didn't receive from God by His grace? Since God has so wonderfully worked in us by His grace, He deserves all the credit!

Do you grasp the importance of what He's teaching us here? Why would I ever compare myself to another by saying, "You know, I am much more patient than he is—I can maintain a peace-ruled heart a lot better than that man." Why would we take the credit for what God has worked into our character by His grace? Neither should I ever say, "You can clearly see that my teaching gift is much more developed and anointed than his; and when it comes to the prophetic, I flow much more proficiently than he does." Since I've received these ministry *gifts* and they're not flowing from me as the source but instead are actually flowing from the Holy Spirit within, why would I ever want or dare to take the credit for His wisdom, power, and grace? The purpose of God is "that the excellence of the power may *be of God and not of us*" (2 Corinthians 4:7).

So over and over in both the Old and New Testaments, we are told this same message in varying ways, "that no flesh should glory [boast] *in His presence*," and "He who glories [boasts] let him glory [boast] in the Lord" (1 Corinthians 1:29, 31). It's very clearly shown in the scriptures that this is a vitally important issue with God! Why?

HIS GLORY COMES IN AS OURS GOES OUT

As we continually yield to God and give Him the glory, the manifest glory can be revealed in ever-increasing ways. God's glory can continue and increase in manifestation to the degree that our glory is going out. Of course, the opposite of that is true as well!

> *The measure with which you glorify God decreases in exact proportion to the measure with which you glorify yourself.* **(AB)**

Glorifying ourselves obviously will decrease the measure of the manifest glory of God.

In 1987 I was teaching in a Bible school in a country overseas that was strong with evangelists but short on Bible teachers. The house was packed, and the people were hungry for the Word of God. I began to teach, the Spirit began to flow, and everyone got very excited. When I ended my message, all the people jumped to their feet and began to cheer and clap their hands. As I walked off the platform and down the middle aisle, suddenly and unexpectedly the Lord revealed my heart to me, and I was patting myself on the back—clearly taking the credit for what the Spirit of God had just done through me. I was so shocked that my knees slightly buckled; and instead of going to my seat, I went out to the janitor's closet. I closed the door, pushed aside the mops and the brooms, and got on my face before God. I said, "God, how long have I been doing that?" He responded back to my heart in a calm and gentle way, "Your whole life."

That one incident has left an eternal impact upon my

life for which I will always be grateful. I learned that the blessing is flowing from His grace, the power is flowing by His Spirit, and it's all to the glory of His great Name! By His grace—Through His power—To His glory!

 Don't put the spotlight on yourself, put it on Him— on His message, His heart, His Name, and His face being projected to others. The goal is that God be glorified! A projector takes an image that others don't see and magnifies that image for all to see. *In our lives, Lord, be magnified and be glorified!*

MINISTERING TO THE GLORY OF GOD

Brother Arthur shares:

> *In my younger days I thought a great meeting was a big crowd, a big offering, and me being the center of attention. Then the Spirit of God began to show me my motive, my conceit, and my efforts to project my own personality.*

> *I was invited to speak at a large meeting, but before I got to the pulpit, the Spirit of God came down on the people. Wave after wave came upon them, and in the midst of it all, I decided to stand up to speak. I opened my Bible and attempted to minister, but instead, I found myself competing with the Spirit of God. An elder pastor sitting*

behind me on the platform pulled the coattails of my jacket and said, "Sit down. Don't you know the touch of the Spirit of God in a meeting? You are like an entertainer, Arthur. You tell your stories and all you are seeking to do is amuse the people. You don't know what it is to minister to the glory of God."

"Faithful are the wounds of a friend" (Proverbs 27:6). As I look back after all those years since the late 1930s, I thank God for that man. He was a friend who was faithful and wounded me when I needed to be wounded. That's the meeting that changed my life and ministry more than any other. Although I resented being corrected at the time, that correction changed my life, and I thank God for it. A revelation was birthed in me then about ministering to the glory of God. **(AB)**

CONDEMNATION OR CORRECTION?

"There is therefore now no condemnation to those who are in Christ Jesus" (Romans 8:1). We don't stand condemned before God but justified by His grace through our Lord Jesus Christ. But it seems that most modern day Christians reject God's loving correction, mistaking it for condemnation. If I'm blocking the flow of God, hindering the move of His Spirit, heading down the wrong path, please, love me enough to show me! It's amazing how much is said in the Bible about correction and how little it's taught and practiced in most churches. Here are a few of many scriptures on this most important, but often neglected subject.

- Jesus assures us, "As many as I love, I rebuke and chasten" (Revelation 3:19).

- Paul tells us, "Convince, rebuke, exhort, with all longsuffering and teaching" (2 Timothy 4:2).

- "My son, do not despise the chastening of the Lord, nor detest His correction; for whom the Lord loves He corrects, just as a father the son in whom he delights" (Proverbs 3:11-12).

- "He who keeps instruction is in the way of life, but he who refuses correction goes astray" (Proverbs 10:17).

- All God-inspired scripture "is profitable for doctrine, for reproof, for correction" (2 Timothy 3:16).

- "Poverty and shame will come to him who disdains correction, but he who regards a rebuke will be honored" (Proverbs 13:18).

Notice how King David views this whole issue of correction. "Let the righteous strike me; it shall be a kindness. And let him rebuke me; it shall be as excellent oil; let my head not refuse it" (Psalm 141:5). I agree wholeheartedly with David and say, "Amen!" to that. And yet, most people are highly offended if another person offers them loving correction. We are so often easy on ourselves and hard on others.

> *If you correct me, I say, "Why don't you mind your own business? If I correct you, "Well, I'm just trying to be helpful."* **(AB)**

Think this through with me: If I'm moving in the wrong direction, viewing it with a distorted perception, or being lured into a dangerous deception, I really want and welcome the Father's loving correction. I'd rather be lovingly corrected by God, His Word, or via a genuine friend than corrupted or harmed by the devil. Wouldn't you?

If we rise up in resentment and irritability at the hint of correction, could that not be a clear indicator and sign to show us what we really need? Why get so huffy if you're not in need of it? If it didn't apply, you would not be stirred up at all, but instead would see the truth it presented and utter a quiet, "Amen." The more correction hurts and offends you, the more you should see how necessary it really is. Correction is always to our great advantage. Its intention is never to hurt us but always to safeguard and help us.

MY WISDOM TOOTH

When I was nineteen years old I experienced my first impacted wisdom tooth. The first few days the pain was minimal, and I thought that I could tough it out and it would eventually subside and go away. Little did I know! After about two weeks I was at the point of continual and unrelenting torture. One night I had finally come to the end of myself, and at 8 p.m. I called our family dentist and asked him if he could extract that tooth, *now*! I apologized for the late hour and short notice but assured him that I would be forever grateful to him.

By 9 p.m. I was sitting in his dental chair and wanting him to get on with it. *Please, move as fast as possible, sir!* I did not care when he injected me three times with a long needle on a syringe full of painkiller. The only time I was concerned was when he gripped that tooth with his dental pliers and leaned on my jaw with all of his weight. That tooth was proving to be a stubborn rascal. It did not want to let go! Suddenly it popped out in one whole piece and all the throbbing pain and pressure was instantly gone—ah! I had instant relief, and even though the process of extraction hurt, it hurt so good!

So it is with spiritual corrections. The process can seem painful, but in the end it hurts so good. What a good and merciful Father we have! He's always trying to help us, keep us out of trouble, and steer us in the right direction. He will use His Word, His Spirit, a loving friend, angels, dreams, visions, or even a little child to guide and correct us. So don't view correction as a dreaded enemy, but embrace it as a necessary, helpful friend.

THERE'S NO GLORY IN SEEKING YOUR OWN GLORY

Jesus clearly taught us, "Take heed that you do not do your charitable deeds before men, to be seen by them. Otherwise you have no reward from your Father in heaven" (Matthew 6:1). It's always good to check our motives. Are we doing what we're doing for the approval of others? Has our motive been that we be seen, that we be heard, that we be known? Are we doing what we're doing for the status it gives us and for the praises of men? If so, we are obscuring the glory of the One we profess to be serving.

Jesus loved the Pharisees, but He called them out regularly over their hypocrisy; and He cautions us, too, not to do "as the hypocrites do in the synagogues and in the streets, that they may have glory from men" (Matthew 6:2). That's all that they sought, and that's all that they got! They forfeited the honor that could have come to them from God because "they loved the praise of men more than the praise of God" (John 12:43). "If anyone serves Me, let him follow Me; and where I am, there My servant will be also. If anyone serves Me, him My

Father will honor" (John 12:26). I don't understand all the ramifications of what it means to be "honored" by God, but it must be a very desirable thing that comes with an eternal reward!

If we will seek the glory of Him Who has sent us, He in turn will be glorified in our midst, and we will be rewarded with an honor that comes from Him alone. "So to seek one's own glory is not glory" (Proverbs 25:27). Steer clear of that trap!

HE DOES THE WORK— HE GETS THE CREDIT

God, by His Spirit and grace, works in you the desire to do His will, and then He supplies the power and ability to accomplish it! He does the "willing" in you *and* the "doing" in you. "For it is God who works in you both to will and to do for His good pleasure" (Philippians 2:13). Once we realize this, we begin to believe in and totally rely on the God inside us Who is continually giving us the right desires and the enabling grace and power that bring those things to pass! Quite often after I've followed God's leading in a situation and put my trust in His power to bring it to pass, I will say, "Oh God, You're so amazing! Thank You, and all glory be to You, kind Sir!" It makes me want to praise Him, worship Him, and make my boast in Him alone.

It's a very healthy practice for us to regularly realize,

just as Apostle Paul did, that we owe all that we are to the grace of God. "But by the grace of God I am what I am." (1 Corinthians 15:10). This continually reminds us to rely only upon Him; and as we do, His enabling grace continues to flow through, and we delight to glorify and magnify Him. It's obvious when you give Him the glory that He's due, His grace will do the work in and through you. Always remember this helpful warning from Jesus; if you don't, your faith will wilt and shrivel up like a flower in the desert: "How can you believe, who receive honor from one another, and do not seek the honor that comes from the only God?" (John 5:44).

Why are we doing what we're doing? *What* is our real motive? Are we doing it for recognition, status, fame, or awards, or so that others will think highly of us? "Did you see *Me* in that picture? Did you mention *My* name? *I* certainly must deserve some credit!" Do we want to be seen as important in the eyes of others? Are we striving for self promotion? It's so easy to slide off the tracks and fall into the undesirable ditch of being a people pleaser—that's where we do what we do unto men instead of unto God. Is my motive that He be seen or that I be seen? Is it for the fame of His great Name or to establish my own name? Is it to His glory or to my own glory?

CONSIDER THESE THINGS

When it came to God's glory, it was never an issue with Jesus. He could be trusted with all power in the security of His relationship with the Father, always and only seeking His Father's will and glory. **(AB)**

Jesus came to show us Another—His Father—and Jesus did not take the credit for the works that the Father did through His life and ministry. "The Father who dwells in Me does the works" (John 14:10). Jesus lifts up His Father, and the Father is glorified in the Son. Now the Son must be glorified in all the rest of us children! And since it's Christ in us Who's doing the works, He gets all the credit or glory for it. His is the glory forever!

God blesses us and moves through us because He's gracious, not because we've earned it, attained it, or deserve it. If we're not careful, we can slip into deception and think that we're the reason God is moving and things are happening. "Oh, if you want to be where it's happening, come and join us. We're the most anointed group in the area!" We then can inwardly, or sometimes even outwardly, glory in ourselves for what God is doing in our midst by His goodness and grace.

All those who think they're "somebody" will have

to lose their identity in the Body, because God will
not give His glory to anybody. **(AB)**

This was the whole reason why God reduced Gideon's army from 32,000 down to 300. "And the Lord said to Gideon, 'The people who are with you are too many for Me to give the Midianites into their hands, lest Israel claim glory for itself against Me, saying, 'My own hand has saved me'" (Judges 7:2).

God does much with little—little is much with
God. God is big, but big is not always God. **(AB)**

"Oh, they have thousands do they? God must be doing a mighty work there!" Not necessarily. Think of the one Man, our lovely Lord Jesus, who lived a perfectly submitted life to His Father and glorified Him in every way. It was said of Him that so many things were done through this one solitary life that "if they were written one by one, I suppose that even the world itself could not contain the books that would be written" (John 21:25). And yet at the end of His ministry, there were only 120 who esteemed Him and loved Him enough to gather together at His command in the upper room. He was truly "despised and rejected by men," and the majority did not esteem Him (Isaiah 53:3).

THE WEEPING WIGGLESWORTH

The following account was given by Albert Hibbert, a contemporary of the well-known British healing evangelist, Smith Wigglesworth. Various reports have been given that credited Smith with raising between fourteen and twenty-three people from the dead. But Smith knew that he hadn't done it. He had learned what some of the rest of us are beginning to learn: "That we should not trust in ourselves but in God who raises the dead" (2 Corinthians 1:9).

Here's the account[1]:

"Wigglesworth never claimed any glory for any miracle of healing. Only wanting Christ to be seen, he scorned the acclaim of men…. I will never forget the last time I had fellowship with him. We were sitting at the table in his home. It was one week before he died.

Looking at me with tears in his eyes, he said, 'Today in my mail I had an invitation to Australia, one to India and Ceylon, and one to America. People have their eyes on me.' Then he sobbed as if his heart would break.

'Poor Wigglesworth,' he weeped. 'What a failure to think that people have their eyes on me. God will never give His glory to another.'

A week later, Smith passed away. He had no sickness, no pain; he just went home. The doctor upon examining the body said, 'There is no visible cause of death. It is just like a workman coming home from his work, taking off his coat, and settling down to rest.'"

THE BLACK BOX

Picture this in your mind's eye—you are walking by the window of a jewelry shop, and suddenly the most beautiful pearl that you have ever seen captivates your attention.

> *We are like the black box that holds the pearl in the window of the jewelry shop. The box doesn't distract or draw attention to itself. It's a background for the glory of the Pearl. Everyone has their eyes on the Pearl!* **(AB)**

> *What a wonderful thing when people will not see me, but will see through me and see God. What a triumph of grace when others will not see the earthen vessel, but the glory it contains, that altogether lovely One. This is the purpose and the plan of God.* **(AB)**

INDIA—THEY TRIED TO WORSHIP US!

On one of our trips to India we went into some villages that were way back in the bush country. I seriously thought we might see some tigers cross in front of us on the bumpy roads we were traveling. The people in those villages had never seen foreigners. At one of our ministry stops, nearly the entire town came—about five thousand people. As we stepped out on the platform that first night, we heard a loud gasp released by the entire crowd, followed by buzzing chatter. I asked our interpreter/guide, "What's going on with the people?" He said, "They think you are angels." Well, consider this with me, the average male there was 5'2". I'm 6'2" and had two guys on my team who were 6'6" and 6'9". These villagers had never seen white people. Plus, they have a solid belief in the realm of spirits. When you add all of that together, it's understandable that they actually thought we were angels!

Through the interpreter, I introduced my team and told them we were men and women from the other side of the world. We had come to bring them the greatest news this world has ever heard! I told them about the Creator God Who loved this world so much that He sent His Son to rescue and redeem us. I told them Who Jesus is, what He did, and that He was present with us to save, help, and heal them; and they believed all that was said!

For the next three days we loved and ministered to those dear people, and Jesus healed them of a large number of diseases and physical problems. The blind received their sight and the deaf their hearing. We even had one lady healed of elephantiasis. When she came to the meeting, she had one normal, thin leg and one diseased leg that looked like the leg of an elephant. We prayed the prayer of faith for her, and Jesus healed her and reduced that leg to its normal size! "Ah, Lord God! Behold, You have made the heavens and the earth by Your great power and outstretched arm. There is nothing too hard for You" (Jeremiah 32:17).

When it came time to leave that village, the people came out and gave us tear-filled, heartfelt goodbyes. Then they fell at our feet and began to worship us! This shocked me and gave me the wrong kind of chill bumps. I grabbed the interpreter and through him told the people to stand and lift their hands to the Almighty God and His Son Jesus Christ. I told them to always remember that He is the One who did all these things, and He alone is to be worshiped forever.

THE EVERLASTING GOSPEL

Years ago a friend of mine, who is also a Bible teacher, said, "What is the everlasting gospel that the angel proclaimed in the Book of Revelation?" I shrugged my shoulders and waited as he turned in his Bible to the scripture: "Then I saw another angel flying in the midst of heaven, having the everlasting gospel to preach to those who dwell on the earth—to every nation, tribe, tongue, and people—saying with a loud voice, 'Fear God and give glory to Him, for the hour of His judgment has come; and worship Him who made heaven and earth, the sea and springs of water'" (Revelation 14:6-7). Our lives are to be wrapped up and spent around those three activities—fear God, give glory to Him, and worship Him. To what degree is the current church promoting, proclaiming, and practicing those three important things? Since these three things are emphasized and declared to be "The Everlasting Gospel," we the church should place a very high value upon them. "Now to the King eternal, immortal, invisible, to God who alone is wise, be honor and glory forever and ever. Amen" (1 Timothy 1:17).

CHAPTER 4
HOW HAVE THE MIGHTY FALLEN?

As you exalt Jesus, you can expect the anointing.
As you exalt yourself, you can expect to lose it.

–Arthur Burt

THE YEAR WAS 1987, and I had just moved my family to Kingston, Jamaica, to help a missions group get a new Bible training center started. A week before the school started, I had decided to spend some time with the Lord in fasting and prayer. The big question on my heart was this, *Why were we seeing so little of the movement of God in our midst?* Others had prophesied of a great move of the Spirit of God that would soon come on the scene. Where was it? What was holding it up?

I vividly remember the night of August 18, 1982. I was preaching in a school auditorium, and at the end of my message, the longest prophecy that I have ever given came forth. Here is about 25 percent of that prophetic word.

THE DAYS OF MY GLORY: "For the days of My glory are far, far from over, says the Lord. The days of My manifesting My Presence and divine might are far from over. The day of My expressing Myself and My power for My Name's sake are far from over; and this generation has merely seen the beginning of the outpouring of the might and the power and the dominion of My Kingdom for My Name's sake, says the Lord. You shall see My power. You shall see My might, and My Name shall be exalted across the world and in the heavens, says the Lord. I am the Lord God Who in might, and Who in dominion, and Who in power, shall show My glory forth in these end days; and those who are bound, and those who are jailed, and those who are in sickness, and those whom Satan has bound, know that when My church shall pray as such and exalt My Name and give glory to Me—and glory I am due—I will move forth by My angels and by My Spirit and I will deliver them. For the days of My outpouring of My glory are far from over; and yea, even the day of this mighty end-day outpouring is at hand. If you will maintain walking in love and coveting the gifts, and praying without ceasing, and walking in love as a body, in unity, and exalting My Name, you'll bring forth that glory and you'll see that glory. For My glory is being outpoured more and more and more and more in these end days. So look for it, expect it, and bless My Name, and it shall come forth even as I have said, says the Lord. You'll see My glory manifested in you, in the earth, in the church, before all flesh."

THE ANSWER SURPRISED ME

So during my time of fasting, I was asking, "Where, oh Lord, is Your manifest glory that so many of us have prophesied about? What is blocking it and holding it back?" Of all the places in scripture to which God could have taken me, He took me to Leviticus, Chapter 10. What happened there was this: After listening to long, detailed instructions from God on how to minister and present offerings to Him, two priests do it their own way and offer "strange/profane" fire before the Lord. Their fall was immediate and decisive as fire went out from the Lord, and they died there.

As a result, God said, "By those who come near Me I must be regarded as holy; and before all the people I must be glorified" (Leviticus 10:3). It was as if God burned the last half of that verse on my heart and mind with a branding iron! "Before all the people I must be glorified." For weeks it revolved around and around inside of me, and I could not connect the dots on how that related to my question, "Where is Your manifest glory and a greater move of Your spirit? What is blocking it and holding it back?" "Before all the people I must be glorified," He would say. And I would respond back with, "I know You should be glorified, Lord! But I don't see how that is at all relevant to Holy Spirit movement and manifestation."

A LATE EIGHTIES LANDSLIDE

If you will go back into church history to about 1986, a massive number of ministers were experiencing moral failures that resulted in the collapse or near collapse of their churches and ministries. Ministers were being caught in sex scandals, having affairs—heterosexual and homosexual, divorcing their spouses, and shattering their families. Ministers were being arrested and going to jail for financial fraud and misuse of funds. Buildings that were used for churches, offices, and Bible schools either went into foreclosure or were put up for sale. This affected the entire church world, not just the Charismatic/Pentecostals.

A study conducted by the Francis A. Schaeffer Institute of Church Leadership Development compiled research from 1989 to 2006 focusing on Reformed and Conservative Evangelical pastors. It found that 40 percent of the pastors had sexual affairs, 31.75 percent had sex with a church member other than their spouse, and 1,500 pastors were quitting the ministry every month.[1]

I remember reading a sad testimony by an Evangelical pastor who was about my age. He had two master's degrees from a major seminary. He committed adultery with a teenage girl in his church and lost his wife, daughter, friends, and his position as a pastor. Because of his crime of having sex with a minor, he was serving a six-year sentence in a federal penitentiary.

WHY DO CHRISTIANS FALL?

Thousands of God's people have fallen. Were these people the "scum" of the Body of Christ? Were they simply the "dirty, rotten scoundrels" of the church? Why did they drop like shooting stars and suffer such disastrous falls? Some say people fall because of weakness, but weakness is never behind a fall. In fact, the Apostle Paul said God's strength is made perfect in our weakness (2 Corinthians 12:9). Some say we fall because we don't have enough knowledge. Until Jesus came to the earth, King Solomon was said to be the wisest person on the earth, and he had a drastic fall. Others say that the fallen one obviously had a "darker" side that no one knew about. But the Apostle Paul said that in our flesh "nothing good dwells" (Romans 7:18). We can walk in the Spirit and not fulfill the lust of the flesh (Galatians 5:16). Still others say, "He was simply overcome by the powers of the devil!" They make it sound like the fallen one was the helpless victim of a demon with overwhelming power. But God enables us to stand against the wiles of the devil (Ephesians 6:11).

GOD WAS TELLING ME THE ANSWER

So as thousands of ministers were falling like dry leaves from a tree in late autumn, God was speaking to me the answer. *Why no sustained move of the Holy Spirit? Why so little manifestation of the glory of God? Why were so many ministries failing?* Notice this: King Herod sat before the people on his throne and received their praise as they kept shouting, "The voice of a god and not a man!" And he immediately fell and died a horrific death "because he did not give glory to God" (Acts 12:23).

Like a broken record this continued to play over and over in my mind, "And before all the people I must be glorified…. And before all the people I must be glorified…. And before all the people I must be glorified." Little did I know that I was about to connect with a man sent by God whose whole message and entire ministry were centered upon the glory of God!

CHAPTER 5
CATCHING THE SPIDER

You need to stop dusting the cobwebs—
go to their source and catch the spider.

–Arthur Burt

WHO?

NOW IT'S APRIL of 1987, and for four months I have been hearing in my spirit, "Before all the people I must be glorified." I've quit telling the Lord, "I know that," and I've figured out that there must be a lot about this glory issue that I don't know. I was expectant and ready to get some answers from the Lord, but little did I know that He was about to release a dump truck load of revelation on me!

The president of our Jamaican Bible school approached me with excitement in his eyes and said, "I just heard that Arthur Burt is on the island and is coming to teach in our school next week!"

I responded with, "Arthur who?"

"You've never heard of him?" he said. "Arthur was

a contemporary of Wigglesworth. He gives people the straight-up, unvarnished truth; he does not sugar coat anything and is not a man-pleaser."

"Well, that's how I like it!" I said. "I like teachers who give a strong, clear word and don't beat around the bush."

FULL OF FIRE AND LIGHT

So our first meeting with Arthur Burt began. I noticed him when he came into the auditorium. He was wearing a pale yellow shirt, stood about 5'8", and was somewhat hunched over in his posture. I saw a man who was very British, with drooping eyelids and a slight smile on his face. When the lively Jamaican praise and worship music started, Arthur took a tambourine and began to play it and dance before the Lord. I noticed his tambourine had little stick-ons all over it—it was covered with yellow smiley faces and phrases like, "Jesus is Lord" and "God loves you."

When he was introduced and invited to come up on the platform, he didn't walk up the steps, he leaped up from the bottom to the top! "Oh, hallelujah! Hallelujah!" he shouted, "I'm seventy-five years old, and I've never been more excited and in love with Jesus than I am right now!" Then he began to jump up and down on the platform like a young man full of glee. I immediately said within myself, "When I'm seventy-five, I want to be just like that!"

LAYING THE AXE TO THE ROOT

Arthur introduced his topic: "God has promised and prophesied, 'But truly, as I live, all the earth shall be filled with the glory of the Lord' (Numbers 14:21). And yet, we see people and ministries all over the earth experiencing great falls. Why? Some would say it's because the church has a sin problem, but sins are simply the fruit of a deeper problem. Sins are symptoms from another source. It's time, my brother and my sister, to lay the axe to the root. If you want to get rid of a rose bush, you don't prune and cut back the branches. That bush will come back with a flourish! You dig it up from the root. Trying to deal with sins is like cutting back the branches.

"Or, take house cleaning for instance—you look in the corners, around the paintings, up in the rafters, and you discover you have a problem with cobwebs. You can dust down the cobwebs, that's true; but in a month or two they're right back there again. What you need to do is to locate and catch the spider.

"The church has been cutting back the branches. It needs to go to the root! The church has been dusting down cobwebs. It needs to catch the spider!

"What is the spider? What is that damnable root from which the fruit of every category of sin springs forth?

Well, it's what originated in the heart of Lucifer. It is that awful thing—PRIDE!"

IS THAT TRUE? LET'S INVESTIGATE

When Arthur said that pride is the root out of which all sins spring forth, my head said, "No!" Deep inside me, my spirit was agreeing and telling me to check out what Arthur had just said. For the rest of the week, Arthur taught us what pride looks like, how it's the enemy of God's glory, and how to deal with it so God can be glorified in and through His church.

In the rest of this chapter I am going to compact much of what I've learned about this many-headed monster that we call pride. My desire is to help you quickly recognize it each time it raises up one of its ugly heads. Let's begin to peel back some of the layers of this onion of pride.

WHAT OTHERS HAVE SAID

- "Pride ... is the root of every sin and evil.... Evil can have no beginning but from pride and no end but from humility."[1] **Andrew Murray**
- "It was through pride that the devil became the devil. Pride leads to every other vice. It is the complete anti-God state of mind."[2] **C.S. Lewis**

- "Pride is the citadel and summit of all evils."[3]
  Theophylact, Archbishop of Bulgaria 1090 AD
- Augustine, Aquinas, and Dante all characterized pride as the ultimate sin.
- "If I only had one sermon to preach, it would be a sermon against pride."[4] **G.K. Chesterton**

WHAT THE SCRIPTURES SAY

"Pride goes before destruction, and a haughty spirit before a fall" (Proverbs 16:18). We know the originator of pride is Lucifer, who also has the distinction of being the first created being to ever take a fall. We know the Bible says he was perfect until iniquity was found in him, and the root of that iniquity was pride. He no longer was content to be under God's loving authority, so he set out to exalt himself above God and to be his own "god." He thought he would be better off if he was independent from God. As Arthur so aptly puts it, "His uprising was his downfalling!" "For you have said in your heart: 'I will ascend.... I will exalt my throne above....' Yet you shall be brought down" (Isaiah 14:12-15). That is exactly what happened as Lucifer fell like lightning from heaven. So pride was birthed by Lucifer, and from then until now it continues to be the source and root cause of every person's fall.

- "A man's pride will bring him low, but the humble in spirit will retain honor" (Proverbs 29:23).
- "When pride comes, then comes shame; but with the humble is wisdom" (Proverbs 11:2).
- "And whoever exalts himself will be abased, and he who humbles himself will be exalted" (Matthew 23:12).
- "Exalt the lowly, and abase the exalted" (Ezekiel 21:26).
- "The fear of the Lord is to hate evil; pride and arrogance … I hate" (Proverbs 8:13).
- "Though the Lord is on high, yet He regards the lowly; but the proud He knows from afar" (Psalm 138:6).

"Rebellious pride which refuses to depend on God and be subject to Him, but attributes to self the honour due to Him, figures as the very root and essence of sin."[5] His manifest glory will depart and stay far away from those who exalt themselves!

MASTER OF THE MASQUERADE

Pride seems to be able to present itself in a thousand different disguises, but that should come as no surprise. Its originator has crafted the art of deception, and pride is the biggest lie in the universe!

Pride says, "I don't need God. I can get along fine by myself!" It's the treason of the creature against the Creator. Pride refuses to rely on God, and that's why it always leads to a failure.

Christ died in my place, but pride wants to rule and reign in the place of Christ. It wants to take His place and be glorified itself! Pride is the worship and exaltation of self—living life more occupied with yourself than with your God—living life with the focus on yourself.

BY DEFINITION

In defining pride, we can say it's a high opinion of one's merit or superiority. Pride is having a lofty opinion of one's self. Vanity, vainglory, self-admiration, conceit, and egotism are all various ways to describe the many faces of pride. Pride wants to show itself preeminent and above others: "I will exalt myself above." Social scientists tell us that most humans are subject to the "above-average effect," where we overestimate our ability and see ourselves as better than others.

- "How can that man be such a popular speaker in the Body of Christ? My Bible knowledge and anointing far exceeds what I hear coming out of him; and besides that, he borders on being boring!"

- "Look at that woman they've put up there to sing! Her musical pitch is a little off. She's overweight and fits into that dress like a stuffed sausage. I've always wanted to sing on stage. Everything about me far exceeds that woman."

- "Well, if you want to go to the best church in town, come to our church. We are where it's happening! We are the biggest church and by far the most anointed."

When David slew Goliath and the Israelite army rode back into town victorious, the women danced and sang, "Saul has slain his thousands, and David his ten thousands" (1 Samuel 18:7). King Saul allowed his heart to be overwhelmed by pride; and from that moment on, he looked at David with jealousy and envy. Instead of maintaining a heart of humility, he let pride rage in his heart until it brought about his ultimate downfall. This is a sad contrast to the situation earlier in his life when, while in a state of humility, Saul was anointed by the Lord and placed as king over Israel (1 Samuel 15:17).

We must guard our hearts and not fall into that "comparison trap" of pride like multitudes of people have done for thousands of years. "But they, measuring themselves by themselves, and comparing themselves among themselves, are not wise" (2 Corinthians 10:12).

A TALE OF TWO HEARTS

In Luke 18:9-14, Jesus gives us the classic parable of the Pharisee and the tax collector. He makes a vivid distinction for us between the heart that receives grace and the heart that doesn't.

The Pharisee had his eyes upon himself—"I am not like other men…. I fast…. I pay tithes." The truth of the matter was that he *was* like other men; we are all in need of the grace of God! Notice that his trust was in himself, and he looked down on others—actually despised others. He puts down others in order to lift himself up. (A little side note here: People try to make sarcasm acceptable by calling it "humor," but pride is at its root. Sarcasm puts down others, laughing at them as it does so; and, in the process, puts itself above the one that it's cutting down.) This Pharisee's confidence and focus is upon himself, not God and His grace and glory. He's more occupied with himself than with God and is actually boasting and congratulating himself for who he is and what he's done. He wants to be seen as important and is seeking the recognition and honor of men. This type of inflated self-love never gets enough attention and always welcomes flattery. The more self-centered a person is, the more critical they are of others. The less selfish they are, the more considerate they are of others. This Pharisee was proud of himself, trusted in himself, and was full of himself. As C.S. Lewis said, "There is no fault of which we are more unconscious in ourselves, and probably conscious of in others, because pride by its very nature is deceitful."[6]

Well pride stinks doesn't it? This man doesn't even know he has it! It's like bad breath. He needs to humble himself and put the "mint" of humility in his mouth. On the other hand, the tax collector does not try to commend or flatter himself before God or others. He does not compare himself with others—makes no mention of anyone else. He places no confidence in himself. He fully owns the truth that he is in sin and in need of God's mercy. He simply utters a heartfelt prayer of seven words: "God, be merciful to me, a sinner!"

The truth of the matter is that *both* of these men were in sin and in need of the mercy and the grace of God. The tax collector left receiving mercy and grace. The Pharisee left deceived and without it. Jesus ends this parable by telling us that everyone who exalts himself (makes himself high/great) will be abased (brought down/fallen), and he that humbles himself (bows low) shall be exalted (lifted up and honored).

ANTI-LOVE

We know from scripture that God is love—that's His nature and that's what motivates Him. God's kind of love is selfless. Its freedom is in the fact that it has no self-focus at all! Its focus is upon the objects of its love.

This is true humility, which has no self-consciousness in it at all. A humble lifestyle is not living in a state of continually demeaning yourself. Jesus lived a humble lifestyle, was sinless, and had more joy in His life than anyone on earth! (See Philippians 2:8 and Hebrews 1:9.)

On the other hand, pride is living life more occupied with yourself than with God—with your will than His will, and your desires than His desires. It's living life with the focus on yourself. All such self-focus is pride. We have a beautiful description of the God-kind of love in 1 Corinthians 13:4-7. It is not puffed up, arrogant, inflated with pride. It does not seek its own—it's not self-seeking, and love does not take offense. Of course, pride is all of these things—the exact opposite of selfless love.

PRIDE IS NEVER HAVING TO SAY, "I'M SORRY"

The love of self—which the world advocates—is a "luxury" that none of us can afford. It is the complete opposite and is diametrically opposed to the God-kind of love. A person caught up in the web of self-love has a hard time saying, "I'm sorry. I was wrong." Whenever there's a conflict or misunderstanding, a self-loving person will always wait for others to come to them and ask for forgiveness. Self-love is quick to blame others, defensive when corrected, and wounded any time it perceives it could have been slighted.

So since people in pride seldom, if ever, say they're sorry, what is behind their thinking? "I never make a mistake. I live a flawless lifestyle. In relating to others, I am impeccable—perfect. All of my attitudes, judgments, and decisions are always right. Wrong? Who, me? Never! It's always the other person's fault. It's never mine!" I actually had a husband tell me once that he never said "sorry" because he was never wrong; and he actually believed that! When I laughed at what he said, he wondered what I was laughing at. I felt so sorry for his wife. To a person in pride, it's always the other person's fault.

BASKETBALL AND THE COACH

Before I was born again at age seventeen, my god was sports—football, basketball, baseball. I played continually from one season to the next—nonstop. When I met my wife and we began to date, here's what I told her: "Sports are first with me; and if you and I are going to get along together, you're going to have to understand that sports come first and you fall into line behind them." Pretty brazen, huh? My identity was wrapped up in a false god and so was my pride.

I supernaturally met Jesus before my senior year, but my one burning desire was to get a basketball scholarship and play in college. My coach told me at the start of the season, "If you play my style of ball, I will make sure that you get a scholarship." I was the only returning starter from the year before, so I was chosen to be captain of the team. Everything was looking very promising, or so I thought. You see, my coach had a very different style of basketball. For instance, we were instructed before one game not to shoot the ball until we heard his whistle. Even if we had a wide open, uncontested shot, we couldn't shoot. We had to keep passing the ball. It resulted in a very boring, low-scoring style of play. In the locker room before the start of another game, he told us, "Tonight, I just want John to shoot the ball. Look for ways to get him the ball." John was a promising young player, but this sounded ridiculous to all of us seniors on the team. We looked at one another in amazement!

The season began to disintegrate from bad to worse, and so did my attitude. There is such a thing as nonverbal communication, and mine was screaming loudly at my coach! I am sure he knew how thoroughly disgusted I was with him. The season ended, and we had a losing record—failures. This was the first losing basketball team I had ever played on in my life, and it felt horrible. To make matters worse, not one college team in all of the USA offered me a scholarship.

At the end of the season, we had our traditional awards banquet. I had also been a captain on the football team and received an award for that, so when the captain's award was about to be announced for the basketball team, I started for the front to get my plaque. Lo and behold, the basketball coach gave it to another player! I couldn't believe it! In my mind that was the ultimate insult, and my pride was hurt to the max. In my heart I wrote him off and washed my hands of him. I decided then and there that I would have nothing to do with him from then on.

Here's how bad I allowed it to get. Baseball season is right after basketball season. During one game as my team was at bat, I was standing in the fenced-in dugout area with my back to the spectators. I suddenly heard my basketball coach right behind me on the other side of the fence. He was speaking to me kindly, asking me how I was doing and trying to joke with me in a light-hearted way. I literally ignored him, treated him like a dead man, and didn't even acknowledge his presence! I don't know how I could have been any more unmerciful to that man unless I had killed him right there on the spot!

Of course, when you refuse to humble, you will try to justify yourself by believing lies like, "Well, he deserves it. He didn't keep his word to me and didn't give me my rightful honor. He should be glad that I don't turn around and spit in his face!" You might be asking, "Are you sure you were a born again follower of Jesus at this point of your life?" Yes! I had been genuinely born again for about nine months. You see, even though the love of God has been poured forth into our hearts (Romans 5:5) and the Word tells us clearly to forgive one another just as God because of Christ forgives us (Ephesians 4:32), we can always choose to reject truth; but we always misrepresent Christ when we do. Do you think that coach had any idea that nine months earlier I had a radical encounter with Jesus and that the very fiber of my being was radically changed forever? I doubt it!

Well, I graduated, married my high-school sweetheart, and forgot about the basketball coach. Four years later, my doorbell rang and in walked three former teammates who played on that same basketball team with me. We all began to reminisce about our senior season, and as they put down the basketball coach, I found myself chiming in with them as well. Right in the middle of a sentence, I heard the Holy Spirit say inside of me, "You thought you had forgiven that coach, didn't you?" Internally I responded, "Yes, Lord, but I guess I haven't." Suddenly I knew in an undeniable way that I was supposed to go to that coach and ask him to forgive me for my bad attitude. Believe me, I did not want to do that. I said again internally, "Lord, I don't know how to contact him; but if You'll set it up, I give you my word, I will do it."

About a month later, I was sorting through the daily mail and saw a letter addressed to me with my high school team logo on it. I opened the letter, and here's roughly what it said: "You are cordially invited to what we hope will become an annual Arvada High School tradition. We want to honor all of our alumni who have played on any of our athletic teams since the start of our school in 1908. We will honor all of you who attend at half time of our basketball game on such-and-such date." So God came for my words, and the question now was whether I would humble. I had a few weeks to pray, and here's what I felt God instructed me to do: Totally take the blame for where you were wrong. Don't bring up anything that he did wrong, and where you see your opportunity to talk with him face to face, go for it instantly!

I went to the game, and it was a good crowd. At half time the announcer said over the PA system, "We are honoring tonight every former player who has played here for the last 66 years. Would you please stand now." Would you believe it? Only one other player stood with me. He was a football player two years my younger, and I had heard that he had become a Christian, too. I always wondered if he was there to make something right with someone as well.

Well, the second half was played, and my mind was not on the game at all. I couldn't tell you if we won or lost. With about a minute left in the game, I left my seat in the bleachers and positioned myself on the court, right in the path to the locker room. I waited there as the coach shook the hands of the visiting players and their coaches. When he turned around to go to the locker room, he looked totally shocked when he found himself face to face with me. I said to him sincerely, "Coach, I truly have become a follower of Jesus Christ, and I want to ask you, from my heart, to forgive me for the rotten attitude I had when I played for you."

Standing on the basketball court, right in front of that big crowd, the coach threw his arms around me and cried like a baby. He embraced me for a couple of minutes as he sobbed and his body shook. Then he looked at me and nodded, still too touched to be able to speak any words, and walked past me to the locker room. I was amazed! But you know what? I felt so good—for him and for me—and I learned that when you humble, God does not humiliate you. No, no, He pours on you His amazing grace that not only restores you, but has a tremendous effect on others, too.

"FATHER, FORGIVE THEM"

As the rain of sharp, heavy stones began to chip Stephen's teeth and break the delicate bones around his eyes, he cried out with a loud voice, "Lord, do not charge them with this sin!" (Acts 7:60). His heart was just like that of his Lord Jesus when He was crucified. Stephen was filled with the Holy Spirit and enabled to see the glory of God. There's an undeniable connection with the glory of God—the manifest Presence—and a heart that will choose to bow down and commit its cause to Him Who sits on the throne.

We remember back to 1 Corinthians 13:5, which tells

us that love is not offended. This is God's own selfless, secure love. Self-love that is rooted in pride is terribly touchy and easily offended. Let's face it, when we're hurt, it's a clear indicator that it's our pride that's been "hurt." People will read the Bible, listen to thousands of sermons, worship, pray, and still not choose to forgive. They think unforgiveness means that they win and maintain an advantage over their "offender." They justify themselves, even though they're bound up with unforgiveness because they've been "hurt." As A.W. Tozer has said, "The labor of self-love is a heavy one indeed. Think for yourself whether much of your sorrow has not arisen from someone speaking slightingly of you. As long as you set yourself up as a little god to which you must be loyal … how can you hope to find inward peace?"[7]

"Great peace have those who love Your law and nothing shall offend them" (Psalm 119:165, KJV). Brother Arthur began to teach from this verse truths that I had never considered. First, when I'm offended, it's a manifestation of my pride being hurt. Oh, but look—if I will choose to rely on the love of God inside me, I can have a heart that enjoys great peace and live a life that is never offended! I don't always have to be stumbling over the offenses of others. I can live in the Presence of God and let everything that could be offensive flow like water under a bridge. If someone says or does something to offend me, I can say, "Father, be merciful to them" and

lay what they've said or done at His feet without brood-
ing over it.

> *Whenever I take offense, I'm always wrong at that*
> *point. Until I come to grips with that issue, I*
> *forfeit the Presence of God in my life.* **(AB)**

It is pointless to try to enter the Presence of God
while holding unforgiveness, hatred, or bitterness in
our hearts toward another. Remember, we want to discover and effectively deal with what hinders the manifest Presence of God in our lives—both individually and
corporately. We don't just want an occasional visitation
of the manifest Presence—we want a continual, constant
manifestation!

THE PUFF/CRUSH PRINCIPLE

I had never heard of the puff/crush aspect of pride until
I met Arthur Burt.

> *Anyone who understands knows that the*
> *inferiority complex is related to the superiority*
> *complex. If you're crushed or hurt when you're*
> *ignored, unrewarded, and left out, to that same*
> *degree, you will be puffed up when you're*
> *recognized, rewarded, and included. This is pride*
> *in two different forms. Pride is manifested in puff*
> *and crush. There is often an immense struggle*

> *going on within anybody when they are left out.*
> *Very few Christians can bear to be slighted. They*
> *get hurt, offended, and upset, not understanding*
> *that until you can sweetly bear having nothing,*
> *you cannot bear something to the glory of God.*
> **(AB)**

So let's hold up this coin of pride and look at both sides of it. Tails first. Pride demands attention and craves the praise of others. So if it's overlooked, not noticed, and gets no honor, it's hurt. We should do what we do to the glory of God and because of our love for Him. But when your advice is disregarded, your opinion ridiculed, and you're left out on purpose, don't let any of that get under your skin. Stay sweet and happy that Jesus loves you! We always need to remember to pour out appreciation, gratitude, and thank you's to each other constantly; but when that's not reciprocated, we can always fall back on this: "Well, I did it to help others and that God would be glorified, so I'll rest and be happy with that motive."

Mark this down in your heart—if I'm crushed when I'm left out, I'm going to be puffed up with pride when I'm honored. These are simply two sides to the same coin of pride. If I learn to handle, to the glory of God, being left out, then I can handle, to the glory of God, being recognized and honored. The bottom line is this: We must readily and rightly give honor to whom honor is due (Romans 13:7), but we mustn't covet and live for the honor that comes from men, but rather for the honor that comes from God (John 5:44).

Let's flip the coin over now and look at the heads side—the puffed up, swollen head of pride. When a person moves into this side of pride, their chest will swell out and their head will puff up. They want to be seen as important … more important … most important!

> *Here comes the danger point—instead of the man seeing God in what he is handling, he sees himself. Instead of 'God is using me,' it's 'god is using ME!' Notice the focus and the emphasis of the heart—'It happened when I prayed! It happened when I laid hands on people! I led him to the Lord. I wrote the book. I … I … I … I, instead of God, it's me.'* **(AB)**

The God-kind of love does not parade itself, is not puffed up, and does not put the spotlight on itself. Pride, on the other hand, will promote itself and congratulate one's self for or because of something one is, or has, or has done. Pride will go to work on carnal objects— physical beauty, riches, intellectual prowess, skill; or it will work on spiritual aspects—spiritual gifts, ministry gifts, or fruits of the Spirit that have been developed in a person's life. Many Christians flow and minister in their gifts to be thought well of by others; and in doing so, they exalt themselves instead of Christ Himself. Remember, spiritual gifts have come to us from God.

They don't originate with us, and every gift is like the sun—it ministers for the benefit of others. If you find yourself focusing on yourself—on your spiritual attainments, giftings, and anointing—applauding and congratulating yourself on who you've become—throw that spider of pride down and stomp on it! Zaccheus climbed up the tree to see Christ, but pride will climb the tree so that it can be seen by others.

True worship is the bowing of self and the lifting up of God. Whenever we are granted glimpses of worship in heaven, we always see that the twenty-four elders are bowing down to Him Who sits on the throne. Yet people can become proud over how they worship God. "Didn't we do a good job of worshiping God tonight? Who has better singers and musicians than we do? We must be the most anointed band in this area! Aren't we a great group of worshipers?" It's right to show people loving appreciation when they glorify Him with their God-given gifts, but "Not unto us, O Lord, not unto us, but to Your name give glory" (Psalm 115:1).

Proud of how you worship God? Lucifer was a worship leader. This archangel was appointed and anointed to cover the throne of God and lead others in worship to God. Lucifer twisted and perverted his God-given beauty, gifts, and abilities, and he fell on the issue of pride. Lucifer was told, "Your heart was lifted up because of your beauty" (Ezekiel 28:17). Pride is the exaltation of self. Humility is the bowing of self and the exaltation of

God. A true worshiper is a man after God's own heart. A worshiper of self is a man after his own heart.

> *The measure with which you glorify God decreases in exact proportion to the measure with which you glorify yourself.* **(AB)**

"And before all the people I must be glorified" (Leviticus 10:3). How many times in church meetings do God's people glorify themselves and don't even realize that they're doing it? This is what keeps the glory of God from manifesting! "The lofty looks of man shall be humbled, the haughtiness of men shall be bowed down, and the Lord alone shall be exalted in that day" (Isaiah 2:11). There's not a thing in my life that I can take the credit or glory for, but I can have a joyful heart and be a grateful worshiper of God!

RACE—FACE—PLACE

> *There's pride of race, pride of face, and pride of place.* **(AB)**

Is there anything more ridiculous and absurd than racial pride, or prejudice? None of us had a thing to do with the color or race we were birthed into. The Bible tells us, "He has made from one blood every nation of men to dwell on all the face of the earth" (Acts 17:26). We all have originated from the One God and share the same blood. God values every person on the planet, and the little Sunday school song is so true: "Red and yellow, black and white, they are precious in His sight." So why the Hitler mindset? Hitler said the Nordic/Aryan race was the superior, master race. He believed they were entitled to rule the world because they were superior to all other races.

My generation remembers the Black Power Movement of the late 1960s. One of the things you heard back then was, "Say it loud: I'm black and I'm proud!" Well, it's great to be black, but not great to be proud. Racial pride causes continual conflict and has erected walls of division all over the world. When you make Jesus your Lord and Savior, you enter the Kingdom of God, where there's ONE holy nation; and God's forever family will come "out of every tribe and tongue and people and nation"! (See 1 Peter 2:9 and Revelation 5:9.)

People have had absolutely nothing to do with the country they were born in, their race, their facial features, or whether they are male or female. So why take a superior attitude about any of these things? Why take the male chauvinist attitude and falsely believe that men are inherently better than women, when God says that in His family, there is no distinction between male and female? (See Galatians 3:28.) This, as well, obviously eliminates a superior, feminist attitude that looks down upon all men with disdain.

How about "pride of face?" Every year the red carpet

is rolled out for all the Hollywood "celebrities." Men and women alike step out of their limos, pause, and pose for pictures to be taken from all angles. At one Oscar event, a lady wore a dress valued at 40 million dollars, and another, a pair of shoes worth two million dollars. From the time we are children in elementary school, we often choose our friends simply on the basis of their looks, but aren't you glad that "the Lord does not see as man sees; for man looks at the outward appearance, but the Lord looks at the heart" (1 Samuel 16:7).

History records for us the very sad and unfortunate story of Absalom, one of the sons of King David. "Now in all Israel there was no one who was praised as much as Absalom for his good looks. From the sole of his foot to the crown of his head there was no blemish in him" (2 Samuel 14:25). It's easy to see that if this young man does not diligently guard his heart, he will allow that spider of pride to entangle him in its web and bring him down. Scripture also shows us that he had a magnificent head of hair that he only cut once a year; and when he cut it, it weighed around five pounds! Absalom believed the praise and flattery of the people, exalted himself, and tried to take over his father David's throne. David's men began to pursue Absalom through a forest; and as he tried to escape, his hair caught in the branches of an oak tree, his mule rode off, and he was left hanging in mid-air by the hair of his head. He was found by his pursuers and three spears were thrust through Absalom's heart.

(See 2 Samuel 18:9-15.) Absalom's hair, which was his pride and glory, proved to be his downfall.

When it comes to "pride of place," how many have been able to handle the fame, honor, prosperity, and power that usually come with being promoted into a place of prominence? Take King Solomon as a prime example—promotion comes from the Lord, and God set young Solomon in the place of being king over Israel. Solomon realized his need to rely upon God, so he humbly asked God for a heart of wisdom and understanding, which God graciously gave him. Very quickly, Solomon became known as the wisest man in all the earth. He spoke 2,000 proverbs and wrote 1,005 songs (see 1 Kings 4:32). Kings and queens from all the nations of the earth came to Solomon to hear his wisdom. But he eventually forgot that his position, wisdom, and understanding all came to him from the Lord; and he let fame, his massive wealth, and his harem of 1,000 beautiful women turn his heart away from the Lord. So the wisest man in the beginning ended up being the most foolish man in the end; and the spider of pride has claimed another victim.

THE BROWN RECLUSE SPIDER

What if I pulled open a jewelry box and allowed a recluse spider to crawl up my arm, across my chest, up my neck, and all over my face. If you cared at all for my well being, you would say, "Oh, shake that thing off of you, onto the floor, and get it under containment!" Pride is the worst type of spider in existence and has similarities to the brown recluse. The recluse loves the environment of darkness and does not like to be seen or discovered. It roams about and hunts in the night. It's only about the size of a quarter, but don't underestimate the effects of its bite—its venom is more poisonous than that of a rattlesnake. Upon the initial bite, the victim is completely unaware of it. However, it soon causes death of the soft tissue and can cause the skin to erupt in what is called a "volcanic lesion." In severe cases, gangrene can set into the skin.

It's so wonderful that we can commit our heart and our ways to God, knowing that in His loving care and mercy, He will locate and shine His spotlight on any area of our lives where we've slipped into pride, flushing the spider from the darkness and enabling us to deal with the problem at its root. We can live confidently and joyfully as we walk together with Jesus in His yoke of humility (Matthew 11:29) and, as we do, we will see Him in ever-increasing measures of His glory!

CHAPTER 6
THE DOMINO CLUB

*The more you are consumed with God's glory,
the less you are attracted to the glory of men.*

–Arthur Burt

I HAVE SAID FOR many years that one of the main indicators that the Bible was not written by man is that it doesn't just show you the victories of its main characters, but it also shows you their greatest failures and falls! Someone who wants to impress you will only show you their successes, but someone who wants to help you will show you their falls, too, so that you won't have to make the same mistakes that they did. You have Someone Who cares for you like no other, and He shows you the falls of many in scripture, not to shame them, but to help and save you from the same falls that others have suffered.

Sadly, most people pay little attention to the examples God so clearly gives us in the Bible, so millions continue to fall like those who have fallen before them. Most of us have seen videos of dominoes aligned in such a way that when the first one is pushed over, it sets off a chain reaction that topples all the others. I read recently that the most dominoes ever toppled at one time was 4,491,863. That seems like a phenomenal number, but it pales in comparison to the number of people who have allowed themselves to be moved by pride and have joined that particular "domino club." Just a short list from the Bible would include: Lucifer, Adam, Nadab, Abihu, Saul, David, Solomon, Elijah, Uzziah, Hezekiah, Absalom, Korah, Haman, Nebuchadnezzar, Herod, and Peter. So let's learn what we can from them, safeguard our hearts and the Lord's glory, and keep out of the domino club.

THE DIZZYING DANGER OF SUCCESS

If you'll pay careful attention, you'll notice that people are more susceptible to falls at the height of their success. They rise to the top and then fall to the bottom. They rise to their highest point and then fall to their lowest. Are you more in danger from pride during great times of success or during trying times of failure? Let's face it, if things seem dead, there is no growth and everything is actually in decline—we put no confidence in ourselves—we put all our reliance upon the God who raises the dead! (2 Corinthians 1:9). It's easier to remain humble when you are unknown and have little, but very few have been able to handle the fame, prosperity, and honor that position and success bring. Pride grows and springs up in times of blessing and increase—times when the glory of God is being manifested and miracles are happening. Every minister who has ever fallen has fallen on this issue. This is what has killed all the moves of God in the past. The glory of God will not compete with the glory of man—which is his pride—there the glory of God will not abide.

> *The whole is not having revival, but handling it; not how much of the Presence of God can I have, but how much can I handle to the glory of God. God is calling for a people who can handle the Presence of God to the glory of God!* **(AB)**

SOME WISDOM ON "SUCCESS"

> *Failure and success must both be defined by God. True success cannot be measured by the results we attain. It is measured by our faithfulness. True success is found in faithfully doing the will of God for the glory of God. This should be our only purpose in life and ministry. The only success I now seek is to be faithful, so what I do, I do to the glory of God. If success is not borne to the glory of God, it will bring us down. Consider the tremendous temptations that attend those on whom honor and wealth are bestowed.* **(AB)**

When we declare ourselves successful and others unsuccessful, and then take the credit for what we consider to be our success, our success becomes the actual cause of our failure. Why is success dangerous? Because it can lead to the rising up of our pride. We may forget to whom all credit is really due. It is God who raises us up, not we ourselves. The Word of God challenges us to ask ourselves, 'For who makes you to differ from another? And what do you have that you did not receive? Now if you did indeed receive it, why do you glory as if you had not received it?' (1 Corinthians 4:7). Pride is a substitute for grace because pride does not recognize what it has received by grace. Pride believes it deserves what God has given. Pride is a huge lie. **(AB)**

When our hearts remain in a bowed position, worshiping and glorifying our worthy Father, it is impossible to fall! But beware of the hour of success, promotion, honor—the hour when all men speak well of you. Beware! It's dangerous. That's what I've learned, and that's what I've observed. **(AB)**

A CLASSIC EXAMPLE

One of the most powerful kings in all of history was Nebuchadnezzar, ruler of the ancient Babylonian Empire. He built a magnificent palace for himself, and his hanging garden was one of the Seven Wonders of the World. In Daniel, Chapter 4, the king gives us his own testimony and recounts a lifelong lesson that he learned the hard way—through experience! The testimony begins when he was at the height of success. He was not a God-fearing king before this experience. The king has a dream from God that shakes him up, so he calls in Daniel, who compassionately gives him the right interpretation. Daniel basically tells him that God has raised him up and given him abundance in his kingdom with provision for all, but he will lose his position, along with his sensibility, for seven years "in order that the living may know that the Most High rules in the kingdom of men, gives it to whomever He will, and sets over it the lowest of men" (Daniel 4:17).

Daniel lovingly pleads with the king and counsels him to repent and to be merciful to the poor, so that maybe this decision can still be reversed. Notice the long-suffering nature of the Lord—He gave the king twelve long months to repent and humble himself, but it was all to no avail. We can easily hear the pride that is still resident in the king's heart: "At the end of twelve months he was walking about the royal palace of Babylon. The king spoke, saying, 'Is not this great Babylon, that I have built for a royal dwelling by my mighty power and for the honor of my majesty?' While the word was still in the king's mouth, a voice fell from heaven: 'King Nebuchadnezzar, to you it is spoken: The kingdom has departed from you!'" (Daniel 4:29-32).

That very hour his mind was changed to that of a beast, and he lived out in the fields eating grass like an ox. His hair grew like eagle feathers and his nails like bird claws. Seven years is a long time! I wonder what his family and the counselors of his royal cabinet were thinking all that time. At the end of the seven years, Nebuchadnezzar lifts his eyes to heaven, and his understanding returns to him. Now instead of his heart and mouth being full of himself, he is blessing, praising, and honoring the Most High! The whole point of his ordeal was in order that people may know "that the Most High rules in the kingdom of men, and gives it to whomever He will." In order to accentuate the point, God restored his kingdom to him and his old counselors and nobles actually returned to him. Amazing!

As a result, instead of having his eyes and his focus on himself, the king's testimony ends this way: "Now I, Nebuchadnezzar, praise and extol and honor the King of heaven, all of whose works are truth, and His ways justice. And those who walk in pride He is able to put down" (Daniel 4:37).

WHY LEARN THE HARD WAY?

The prideful fall of Lucifer has set off a continual chain reaction of falls throughout the history of humanity; and yet most people, both Christian and non-Christian, seem to learn absolutely nothing from the tragic mistakes of others. Wouldn't you rather learn from the mistakes of others instead of making the same mistakes yourself? I thank God that He does not cover over the falls of others but shares them with us in His Word so that we can avoid those same traps and pitfalls. I also thank God for His loving, merciful correction. "Moreover by them Your servant is warned, and in keeping them there is great reward" (Psalm 19:11). So let's forever stay aware of the fact that promotion, success, and fame, along with the prosperity they bring, present us with a dangerous combination of challenges.

Here are a few more of many in the Bible who fell prey to pride and joined the domino club. It was said of King Uzziah: "So his fame spread far and wide, for he was marvelously helped till he became strong. But when he was strong his heart was lifted up, to his destruction" (2 Chronicles 26:15-16). We love King David, sweet psalmist of Israel, a man after God's own heart, but he also fell in the midst of success and the ease and luxury it can bring. "Now it came to pass in the spring of the year, at the time when kings go out to battle ... " (2 Samuel 11:1). King David should have been at battle, but he leisurely stayed at home. Did he believe he was better than the others and "deserved" some rest and relaxation? "And from the roof he saw a woman bathing, and the woman was very beautiful to behold" (2 Samuel 11:2). You know the rest of the story. He committed adultery with her and had her husband killed in an attempt to cover up his sin.

How did David falsely reason himself into this tragic situation? Did the enemy present to him thoughts like: "You've worked so hard; you deserve a little pleasure. After all, you're the king of all Israel. Only this one time won't hurt. No one will ever know about it, and God is a God of forgiveness." God is a God of forgiveness, and David was forgiven; but this one act drastically affected his family, sent his ministry into a tailspin, and as far as "no one will ever know about it" goes, you and I are reading about it thousands of years later. And it's the same with the people of God today. Instead of learning from the past experiences of others, we ignore the lessons of history and join the domino club by falling just like they did. The percentage of modern day ministers who have fallen is shocking.

I used to think the root cause of the destructive fall of the city of Sodom was its sins of sexual perversion. Then one day Ezekiel 16:49 jumped out at me and gave me the root reason: "Look, this was the iniquity of your sister Sodom: She and her daughter had pride, fullness of food, and abundance of idleness; neither did she strengthen the hand of the poor and needy." At the top of the list? Pride.

JOHN ALEXANDER DOWIE—A FORERUNNER OF HEALING

Few today remember or have even heard of John Alexander Dowie. He was an Australian minister who came to America in 1888 and left a lasting impact that continues to bear fruit to this day. He was a revivalist and a reformer who began to preach and practice a long neglected aspect of the Great Commission, "They will lay hands on the sick, and they will recover" (Mark 16:18). Dowie established a church in Chicago, along with what he called his "Divine Healing Home." This was simply a building on the church campus where people could come for prayer, the laying on of hands, and teaching from the Bible. Soon Dowie was praying for a thousand people a week with great success.

Buffalo Bill Cody's niece, Sadie Cody, was carried to the Home in a body cast. She was near death and in extreme agony; her family thought she would be brought back a corpse. She had five destroyed vertebrae and an abscess the size of a fist at the base of her spine. Dowie laid hands upon her in the Name of the Lord; she was healed, the tumor disappeared, her mobility returned, and her spine could be rubbed as hard as possible without her feeling any pain. Here are her own words: "I consider Dowie the greatest blessing God ever sent to Chicago. I cannot find words to praise the Lord for what He has done for me. I will give Him my life's service."[1]

Amanda Hicks was the first cousin of Abraham Lincoln. She had a massive internal tumor that had expanded her waist size by six inches. Her friends carefully placed her on a stretcher, and she traveled by train 400 miles to the Divine Healing Home. As the train pulled out of the station, they all wept and thought they were saying their last goodbyes. Dowie prayed for her; she was healed of that cancerous tumor, and over the next few days passed gallons of fluid and tumorous tissue. Amanda then traveled all over America and Europe telling her testimony to the glory of Jesus and His Gospel.[2]

Dowie was a man who was attacked, criticized, and slandered by tabloids; and his life was threatened by murderous mobs on more than one occasion. In 1895 he was arrested 100 times because his Divine Healing Home did not have a "hospital ordinance." He seemed to thrive on persecution and had God's all-sufficient grace for it, but he had no sustaining grace for his ever-growing root of pride.

The ministry of Christ the Healer was being restored to America in the late 1800s, and one of the forerunners, along with John Alexander Dowie, was Maria Woodworth-Etter. The Lord was confirming the healing Word that she preached with the same amazing results that Dowie experienced. In one of her large meetings, a little boy who was blind, deaf, and dumb, as well as quadriplegic, was instantly healed in the presence of all. Dowie cut her down and criticized her publicly on a continual basis because he didn't approve of her style of ministry. In fact, he regularly condemned and harshly judged the ministries of D.L. Moody, R.A. Torrey, and A.B. Simpson, along with a host of others. As you will see in the next chapter, harsh, unmerciful judgments are one of the worst manifestations of pride.

In 1900, at the first of the year, Dowie announced he would build a Christian city and call it *Zion*. He had purchased a ten-square-mile plot of land 40 miles north of Chicago. (Zion, Illinois, is still a town, with a population of 25,000 as of 2013.) It would be against the law to have tobacco, alcohol, drugs, or gambling within the city limits. Many Christians make this common mistake, not realizing it is also rooted in pride. They will make a major decision without seeking any advice from trusted people around them. Then to everyone's surprise, they will confidently announce, "The Lord has told me to do such-and-such!" You can tell by the way they declare it that their minds are already made up. It's as if they've placed an invisible "No Trespassing" sign around them in the spirit realm. I remember the day well when Arthur Burt taught us this valuable truth, and I pray that you, too, will value it and hide it in your heart: "In a multitude of counselors there is safety" (Proverbs 24:6).

Body ministry

Dowie

We can easily forget that the same Holy Spirit that lives in us lives in all our brothers and sisters, too! It's the body of Christ that we are a part of, and no person is an isolated member called to live and move by themselves. Dowie did not operate this way. He had no advisory board—no checks and balances. He took counsel from no one. Zion, Illinois, had no city council. Dowie declared the city a theocracy, but he held absolute sway and control over even the smallest details of the city. In June of 1901, to everyone's shock and dismay, Dowie came out with his most outrageous and fatal declaration. He held a special meeting and declared himself to be "Elijah the Restorer," whose return to earth was prophesied by the Bible prophets of old. Not only would he build Zion, Illinois, but he would establish many cities of Zion throughout the world. Finally, he would purchase Jerusalem from the Persians and Turks, preparing that city for the return of the Messiah. He then had a throne, crown, and priestly robes made for himself! (You can see pictures of this in a few books or on the Internet.)

Understandably, from this point forward Dowie's life and ministry went into a tailspin. For the next five years he determinedly tried to press through and make his vision manifest. He then suffered a debilitating stroke that confined him to a wheelchair. The healer could not heal himself and went into eternity at the age of 60. Well, what good came out of this ministry? Was it all for nothing? No! When Dowie was moving with God, it was God doing the works through him. Multiplied thousands had been saved and healed by the power of God. Here is just a short list of some of the ministers who were raised up under Dowie and came out of Zion, Illinois:

- John G. Lake, who went to South Africa and established 1,000 churches, then returned to America and started his well-known Healing Rooms;
- F.F. Bosworth, who traveled throughout Canada and the USA and wrote his excellent classic book, *Christ the Healer*;
- Gordon Lindsay, who founded Christ for the Nations Bible Institute in Dallas, Texas;
- Charles Parham, who was instrumental in the Pentecostal revival in Topeka, Kansas;
- Raymond T. Richey, who was a healing evangelist.

We can learn from the life of John Alexander Dowie that it's so very important how you finish your life and ministry. "A good name is better than precious ointment" (Ecclesiastes 7:1). "A good name is to be chosen rather than great riches" (Proverbs 22:1). Unfortunately, when we think of Dowie today, we think of his sad and tragic ending. Let's never forget that before all the people, God must be glorified!

The greatest enemy to the glory of God is the glory

of man, which is rooted in man's pride. Pride is man's glory competing with God's glory. **(AB)**

CELEBRITIES

In the little country of Wales, a tremendous move of God took place from 1904-1905 that affected nearly the entire world. Out of the Welsh Revival came two brothers who were mightily used by God as healing evangelists—Stephen and George Jeffreys. Their ministry swept through Wales, Ireland, Scotland, and England, filling the largest halls and auditoriums with thousands of people. Dramatic healings happened everywhere, which led to scores of people finding Jesus as Lord and Savior all over the UK. Arthur Burt was greatly influenced by Stephen Jeffreys and followed him from town to town like a groupie would follow a rock star. On three separate occasions in three different towns, Jeffreys pointed at Arthur out of the crowd of thousands and said, "Young man, God wants you!"—meaning God was calling him into the ministry.

Arthur says, "I was seventeen years old, and I worshiped Jeffreys. I had pin-ups of him on my bedroom wall like teenagers do of Michael Jackson, Elvis, or Marilyn Monroe. Then one day I heard him stand before the people and say, 'The whole world is lying at my feet!' That statement sent a shudder through my whole being. I knew he was finished. Shortly thereafter, he was stricken with severe, crippling arthritis and was confined for the rest of his life to a wheelchair. He was frozen in a permanently bent over position, and in order to look him in the face, you had to get down on bended knee. He couldn't lift up his head."

We help set people up for a fall when we exalt them and place them on pedestals. How many of us have unknowingly contributed to their falls? Satan will gather people around you to lift you up and exalt you because he knows that what goes up, must come down. A celebrity by definition is someone held up for fame and renown. Can you see that we are not to be the celebrated ones, the celebrities? Do we want others to see Him or us? Are we living for the fame of His great Name or to build up our own name?

> We help put the Humpty Dumptys of ministry high up on the wall, and then wonder why they have a great fall! Don't put people on pedestals. There is only one celebrity—Jesus! There is only one wonderful One. **(AB)**

At this point I can almost hear you asking these questions: "Once a person has fallen, can they recover? How does all of this work? How can a person be kept from the falls that so many others have taken?" Before we take a detailed look at how all this works, let's answer the first question by saying, "Yes! A person can recover!"

One of the best examples of a person recovering from a disastrous fall was King David. "So he died in a good old age, full of days and riches and honor" (1 Chronicles 29:28). In the Book of Acts, it is said of David that he found favor before God, and he's still described as "a man after God's own heart" (see Acts 7:46 and 13:22).

THE MECHANICS OF IT ALL

"God resists the proud, but gives grace to the humble.... Humble yourselves in the sight of the Lord, and He will lift you up" (James 4:6, 10).

"God resists the proud, but gives grace to the humble. Therefore humble yourselves under the mighty hand of God, that He may exalt you in due time" (1 Peter 5:5-6).

For some reason, until I met Arthur Burt, I had always thought that these two portions of scripture in the New Testament only applied to the proud *un*believer, not the proud believer. But both James and Peter are writing their letters to Christians. I had failed to see that we *all* have an "Achilles' heel," and if we allow ourselves to be touched there, we will fall down every time. The term "Achilles' heel" means the spot where a person is vulnerable. According to Greek mythology, when Achilles was born his mother dipped him in the River Styx in an effort to make him immortal. She held him by one heel, and the area where her fingers held him remained dry. That was the one area of vulnerability for Achilles, just as pride is the area of vulnerability for every human on planet earth.

THE "MANIFOLD GRACE OF GOD"

God's wonderful grace has many sides and aspects to it. His amazing "saving grace" eradicates our sins and establishes us as citizens in His forever Kingdom. He accepts us as His own sons and daughters, making us the righteousness of God in Christ (2 Corinthians 5:21), all on the basis of saving grace. We could never merit that gift of righteousness, and of course, we can never improve upon it, either.

But there's also "enabling grace," which imparts to you the gifts of the Spirit, ministry gifts, and which enables you to grow in your walk with the Lord. Enabling grace gives you the power to fulfill God's will, and it also gives you the desire to do and the ability to know His will in the first place! God's enabling grace works His wonderful character into your personality, and that grace sustains you and keeps you from falling. Oh, thank You, Lord, for Your lovingkindness and Your all-sufficient grace!

In short, this enabling grace empowers us to fulfill our callings and glorify/honor God with our entire lives. Paul understood and stated it well when he said, "But by the grace of God I am what I am, and His grace toward me was not in vain; but I labored more abundantly than they all, *yet not I, but the grace of God which was with me*" (1 Corinthians 15:10). Paul is not talking about saving grace, that grace that gives you your right standing before God. He is talking about enabling grace, and at any given time in your life you can be experiencing greater or lesser degrees of enabling grace. How so? How can that be? How does that work?

THE ANATOMY OF FAILURE

"God resists the proud, but gives grace to the humble" (James 4:6; 1 Peter 5:5). God will never support with His grace anything that has originated from pride. He will never pour grace into anything that is rooted in pride in order to enable its success. On the contrary, He will withhold grace from it to insure that it does not succeed.

> *Failure is nothing more than a withdrawal of the grace of God on a certain given point in my life.*
> **(AB)**

Why would grace be withdrawn there? Because you've believed a lie from the devil there. You are bowing to the devil there. You've agreed with him and are allowing him to move you into a position that stands in opposition to God and His ways, purposes, thoughts, and will. God will always resist such a position by giving you no "enabling grace" to succeed. Move into pride, you forfeit His grace—failure!

Where there's pride, there's no grace. Where there's grace, there's no pride. Pride is like a valve that can halt the flow of God's enabling grace into any given area of our lives.

> In any area of my life where I'm in pride, the glory, the power, the grace of God will be limited. It's the governing factor—the controlling issue.
> **(AB)**

Is there a place in God's enabling grace where we can walk on the wall of success and not fall? Yes! It's where we, in loving humility, handle all that we've received from God to the glory or credit of God. We delight in a loving and responsive way to continually "fear God and give glory to Him … and worship Him" (Revelation 14:7).

God does not push you into failure and sin. He is not the cause of your fall. He has all the ability necessary to keep us from falling, and He wants us always to walk in victory through our Lord Jesus Christ! (See Jude 24; 1 Corinthians 15:57.) But He will not feed grace to that monster of pride. Grace enables us to stand and not fall. You can do the math. As people persist in pride, stubbornly resisting all of our Father's loving attempts to warn and correct, they eventually run out of enabling grace, and down they go! "Therefore let him who thinks he stands take heed lest he fall" (1 Corinthians 10:12). I can't blame God for my fall. He doesn't push me down!

In fact, it's He who keeps me from falling. But if I rise up in pride and take the credit for what God has been doing in me or through me by His grace, I move out of humility and into that graceless place of pride that always results in a fall.

1 Timothy 3:6 makes it very clear that new believers are especially susceptible to this. They can easily get puffed up with pride and fall like the devil did. We've all suffered falls, before and after we were born again. Then we've asked ourselves, "How in the world did that happen?" Remember how Peter so vehemently vowed that even if everyone else stumbled because of Jesus, he would never be made to stumble: "Even if I have to die with You, I will not deny You!" (Matthew 26:35). You know the rest of the story. Before sunrise, Peter had denied the Lord three times. How did that happen? First of all, Peter compared himself to others and, in effect, said he was better than them: "They may all deny You, but I never will!"

Second, Peter failed to see that it's by our faith grip on God's grace that we are enabled to stand, not by faith in ourselves and our own will power. We all stand by grace, and we all fall without it. Your past failure should give you compassion for others currently in failure—"There go I but for the grace of God." If you see your fellow Christian fall today, always remember what keeps you from falling tomorrow—by grace you stand. "Brethren, if a man is overtaken in any trespass, you who are spiritual restore such a one in a spirit of gentleness, considering yourself lest you also be tempted" (Galatians 6:1). Tempted? With what? With the same thing that brought about your fellow Christian's fall.

There is not a day in any person's life when we are not dependent upon the grace of God to sustain and put us over. It doesn't matter if you've been walking with the Lord for 20, 30, 40 years—you stand by the grace of God alone. Moment by moment your lungs suck in life-sustaining air. In the same way, your faith inhales the sufficiency of His enabling grace. So it becomes very obvious that when a person has been placed in a high and visible position, it requires a great measure of grace to enable that person to stand and maintain a humble heart. Those who have been greatly used in the cause of Christ have learned how devastatingly weak and defeated they become when they cease to totally rely upon Him.

Humility is total dependency upon God. Who did we see in Old Covenant days who was in a high position of authority and experienced the manifest glory of God? Moses. And what did God highlight about Moses? "Now the man Moses was very humble, more than all men who were on the face of the earth" (Numbers 12:3). More than anyone else on the face of the earth! See the connection here. The more you depend upon God and refuse to depend upon yourself, the more you glorify and exalt God and refuse to glorify and exalt yourself, the more God lifts you higher and higher into realms of His grace, power, and manifest glory! Moses was the most humble man on earth in his generation, and he experienced more of God than any other person in his generation. Humility lifts you "from glory to glory." Are you beginning to see that humility has a direct and inseparable connection to the degree that a church or individual is experiencing the manifest Presence of God?

The humble heart fully realizes and gladly confesses, "It's not my power. It's Yours! It's not my name. It's Yours! It's not my glory. It's Yours!" "We have this treasure in earthen vessels, that the excellence of the power may be of God and not of us" (2 Corinthians 4:7). Since our sufficiency is of God, we freely and readily recognize that we have none of our own. This keeps us in a continual state of humble dependence that continually keeps us connected to the all-sufficient grace of God.

RECAP

If we lift ourselves up in pride, we will inevitably experience a fall. If we are in sin, we can apply the blood of Jesus and our conscience can be cleansed. If we are in pride, we can humble ourselves in the sight of the Lord and be lifted right back up again! (See James 4:10.) We never need to remain in despair, constantly beating ourselves up over our past failures. I humble myself "in the sight of the Lord" with my focus ever on His Presence, wanting Him to be seen and exalted, recognizing that He alone is worthy to be praised. Our desire is to see Heaven's atmosphere, His glorious manifest Presence, displayed here upon the earth. The tree, in order to go higher and higher, must ever strike its roots deeper and deeper. The greatest degree of His manifest Presence is reserved for those who realize this! "And He shall lift you up" into greater realms of His glory.

It's true that "all have sinned and fall short of the glory of God" (Romans 3:23), but He did not create us to have a glory-less life! When we live our lives in humility, totally dependent upon Him, we automatically glorify God and keep the gateway open for His glory to manifest upon our lives and in our midst. So let this be the 24/7 declaration of your heart: "Lord, I'm after You, Your glory, and the fame of Your great Name!" And watch how His enabling grace and goodness and His manifest Presence come forth in ever-increasing measure!

CHAPTER 7
TO JUDGE OR NOT TO JUDGE

*The heart may choose to be a god and rise in
pride or humble to God and find grace.*

–Arthur Burt

OUR DESIRE IS to see God glorified and to walk
with Him and enjoy His manifest Presence whenever we meet and wherever we go. Since He will not
release His glory or grace into anything that's rooted in
pride, we need to recognize its symptoms and avoid it
like the plague! Most people are unaware of the fact that
our unrighteous judgments we make regarding others is
one of the most common manifestations of pride. Social
scientists say that most people judge a first acquaintance
within the first seven seconds. What could we possibly
know about the person in that short amount of time?

How are our judgments rooted in pride? Let's break
this down and you'll clearly see it. "Do not judge according to appearance, but judge with righteous judgment"
(John 7:24). Jesus clearly forbids us to judge externally—
according to appearance; we can call that unrighteous
judgment. Take this into consideration: I may see or hear

about what you've done, but I don't know what your motive was. I don't know what you were facing. I lack all the facts, and I may not be totally objective; therefore, it's impossible for me to make a right or righteous judgment. A person with a submitted heart of humility realizes that they don't know the intentions of another person's heart. But how often have you found that people who know the least about you and your situation seem to think they know the most about you, and they don't hesitate to rise up in pride and judge you falsely!

THERE IS ONLY ONE JUDGE

- "For God Himself is judge" (Psalm 50:6).
- "You sat on the throne judging in righteousness" (Psalm 9:4).
- "For the Lord does not see as man sees; for man looks at the outward appearance, but the Lord looks at the heart" (1 Samuel 16:7).

When we don't recognize these things, it's as if we are saying, "God, move aside and I'll render my verdict on this situation. Let me sit on Your throne of judgment!" The Father, Who knows the motives of all hearts, is the only One qualified for the position of Righteous Judge, so don't put yourself in the unpleasant position in which He has to ask, "Who are you to judge another?" (James 4:12).

Look at how Jesus flowed in perfect submission to the

Father in this vitally important area. It was prophesied of Him, "He shall not judge by the sight of His eyes, nor decide by the hearing of His ears" (Isaiah 11:3). That would clearly be an unrighteous judgment. Jesus said, "Don't judge according to appearance, but judge with righteous judgment" (John 7:24). Can you see there are two completely different kinds of judgment, and they originate from two completely different sources? Don't judge this way—it originates from pride; but judge this way—it originates from God.

Jesus would not make His own independent judgments. He had to arrive at righteous judgments by refusing to make external judgments of His own. The same is true and is required of you and me, so pay close attention to what our Lord is teaching us here, please! "I can of Myself do nothing. As I hear, I judge; and My judgment is righteous, because I do not seek My own will but the will of the Father who sent Me" (John 5:30). Jesus clearly said, "As I hear, I judge"—listening for the Father's righteous judgment on the person, place, or thing. Unless the Father spoke to Jesus, He did not judge. As we also keep a submitted heart to the Father, we learn to move in His judgments instead of our own—just like Jesus. A judgment that is righteous must come from God to me and then through me to the person or into the situation.

We are told in the Bible to judge righteously in areas that involve:

Sinful conduct within the Church	1 Cor 5:3, 9-13
	Rom 16:17
	2 Thess 3:6-15
Disputes between Christians	1 Cor 6:1-8
Prophecy	1 Cor 14:29
	1 Thess 5:20-21
False ministers and false prophets	Rev 2:2
	Matt 7:15-20
False doctrine	2 John 9-11

Of course we seek the Lord, hear from Him, and render His righteous judgment in a spirit of meekness and humility. When Jesus said, "Judge not, that you be not judged" (Matthew 7:1), He was not saying that there's never a time to make righteous judgments. We've all seen ridiculous situations in which a person in the church will swindle, lie, or try to sexually seduce others and then say, "Remember, Jesus said not to judge!" No! Jesus said to judge with righteous judgment! Church leaders take note here—if you refuse to administer righteous judgment, you will allow your church to become an unsafe environment—a cesspool of immoral behavior; and the glory of God will soon depart from your midst.

AN INFALLIBLE PRINCIPLE OF GOD

"Judge not, that you be not judged. For with what judgment you judge, you will be judged; and with the measure you use, it will be measured back to you" (Matthew 7:1-2). So Jesus couldn't make this any clearer—judgments that do not originate from God, but originate from us, are unrighteous and forbidden. And yet this is one of the most common and frequent errors we make that allow the spider of pride to spring up and bite us! Notice Jesus said that "with the measure you use, it will be measured back to you." The measure of judgment you release upon another will be the measure that is released back on you. So be merciful, just as your Father also is merciful; because when we withhold mercy and grace from others, we find in that area of our lives that we are without mercy and grace as well (see Luke 6:36-38 and James 2:12-13.) So often we quote Luke 6:38, "Give and it will be given to you," without referring to its context—which is fine in one sense, because Jesus is teaching on the principle of sowing and reaping—but the context in the two preceding verses is this: Don't make your own judgments and condemn people, but instead extend things like mercy, grace, and forgiveness, which would include giving them the benefit of the doubt, because whatever you give out to others is what will be coming back to you. What you give out to others today will determine what you reap back tomorrow. It's an infallible, universal principle that applies to everyone—no exceptions. Those who fail to believe this will soon prove in their own life's experiences that it is absolutely true!

MY BOOMERANG ON THE HIGHWAY

STORY

I lived for ten years in the mountains of Colorado and had to commute nearly every day down the canyon to my office in Boulder. I went through a stretch of time where weekly, and sometimes daily, other drivers would pull out right in front of my car as if I didn't exist. One morning I had not driven two miles from my house when a woman pulled out from a side road right in front of me. Because she was going slowly, I got right up on her bumper and rode it for a few minutes. My wife said to me, "Back off of her! What are you doing? That's dangerous and unlawful!"

I replied in a hot tone of voice, "I want to teach her a lesson and let her know she needs to be more careful!"

We traveled another ten miles and driver #2 pulled out right in front of me without even looking my way. "What's wrong with these people?!" I exploded, "Are they on drugs? They act like they're the only people on the planet and the whole world revolves around them! If that happens one more time, I'm laying on the horn."

My wife said, "Settle down. Maybe they've had a hard morning; maybe they're dealing with some difficult issues in their life; or maybe they have a handicap." She gave them grace and the benefit of the doubt, and, of course, she was right.

As we got closer to the bottom of the canyon, driver #3 pulled directly out in front of me, and I responded with a ten-second blast from my horn. I was true to my word—I really gave it to him and laid on my horn. But I was not true to God's Word. I gave no grace, mercy, or benefit of the doubt to any of these drivers like my wife did. As a consequence, I set into motion the infallible principle of sowing and reaping. Your harvest will depend entirely on what you sow; what you give out to others is what will come back to you. "Do not be deceived, God is not mocked; for whatever a man sows, that he will also reap" (Galatians 6:7). I carelessly threw the wrong kind of boomerang!

Here's what happened—with God, my wife, and the holy angels all as witnesses: When I drove into town just a few minutes later, I stopped at an intersection. I looked to the left, looked to the right, and something I saw distracted my attention just for a couple of seconds. I should have checked to the left again before I pulled out, but I didn't. I pulled out, and suddenly you could hear that awful sound of smoking, squealing tires coming to a desperate halt, accompanied with a long, ten-second blast from the other driver's horn! My wife was so startled she screamed out in terror. We came within inches of a serious collision. Immediately, I humbled myself and said, "Oh, Father God, I am sorry for my irritable judgments on those other three drivers. Bless them, Lord. Continue to protect them today, and thank You for your mercy and grace towards me just now!"

Give people mercy, grace, forgiveness, and the benefit

of the doubt. Isn't that what we all want? "Blessed are the merciful, for they shall obtain mercy" (Matthew 5:7). "Therefore be merciful, just as your Father also is merciful" (Luke 6:36). Whatever we give to others is exactly what is coming back to us—boomerang!

PASTOR ARTHUR AND THE SLEEPY FARMER

When Arthur Burt was a young minister, he pastored a country church in England. It was a small church, and the chapel was heated by a pot belly stove. Pastor Arthur would arrive before the people and get the meeting place warm and toasty. In his congregation was a farmer who was not used to warm and toasty; he was used to being outside in the fresh, crisp air. So here's what happened in every meeting, week after week. When Arthur would begin to preach, this farmer would shout for the first ten minutes, "Oh, yes, Brother Arthur! Amen! Amen! Glory to God!" and then he would fall silent and fall fast asleep for the next forty minutes. Then every week, as if he had an internal alarm clock, he would suddenly awaken and shout, "Glory to God! Amen! Amen!" as if he'd followed the entire message.

Arthur could have submitted this to the Lord and received the enabling grace necessary for the situation, but he didn't. Arthur says, "I began to let it boil in my heart. I determined within myself, if he does it again this morning, I'm going to let him have it!" So, of course, the very same thing happened that morning. As the farmer awoke with five minutes left and began to lift up his voice, Arthur confronted him and said, "Hold it, brother. You're nothing but a big hypocrite! Every week you sleep through most of the message and then wake up like you've followed the whole thing. No, no, that must end now!" Arthur proceeded to chastise, shame, and condemn the farmer in front of the whole church.

I'll let Arthur tell you in his own words what happened after that: "That came out of the irritation of my flesh. It was not a righteous judgment that proceeded from God. It was my own unrighteous judgment. I can't sow my own judgments into other people's lives. We don't know their motives. We don't know all the facts; therefore, we cannot give out our own judgments.

"Here's what I experienced after that—God is my witness—whenever I sat down in a meeting for announcements, a special, testimonies, or another speaker, it was like my eyes would supernaturally close. I could not stay awake! I would lick my fingertips and rub my eyelids; I would literally try to pry my eyes open—all to no avail! And it continued week after week after week, and then—I saw it! I had no grace for that dear brother; now there was no grace for me. And I saw that I would only get grace if I would humble myself. Since I had done this before the entire church, I needed to come before the entire church and make it right—so I did: 'I had no grace or mercy for that man. I was a bad example before all of you. I am sorry.' I went and apologized to the farmer, too, and that broke the cycle that my own judgment had set into motion."

I think so often people mistakenly think the situation they've fallen into or are stuck with is the result of some type of "generational curse" when, more often than not, it's the direct result of an unrighteous judgment we are holding in our hearts against another.

> When you unrighteously, unmercifully judge another, you are condemning yourself. You are like the man in the tree who unknowingly is sawing off the very branch he is sitting on! The man who makes no allowances for others will find none made for him. By your present judgments you're digging your own grave for the future. When you presume to be judge, you father your own failure. **(AB)**

In my own case with the other three automobile drivers, I mistakenly believed that I was different than they are, better than they are, and thought I could never do what they had just done. Pride led me to believe they were inferior to me. Result? I soon found myself doing the exact same thing.

I have had minister friends who marveled and talked incessantly about how they couldn't believe how a fellow minister committed adultery and left his wife. "I would never have an affair like he did," they said. "What was he thinking?" Less than two years later they each did exactly the same thing.

How many are in marital failure today who sat in judgment of others on the same thing yesterday.
(AB)

HAMAN HANGED HIMSELF

This whole story can be quickly read in the Book of Esther. Haman was an advisor to the king who despised a fellow advisor, Mordecai, who was Jewish. So Haman deceitfully devised a plan to eliminate all Jews and got the king to approve it. Haman then built a gallows for Mordecai that was 75 feet high. He had determined to publicly destroy him and put him to shame before everyone! But through a quick turn of events, Haman's intentions backfired on him, and the unrighteous judgments he had decreed on Mordecai came right back upon him. He was hanged on the very gallows that he had prepared for another. "Whoever digs a pit will fall into it, and he who rolls a stone will have it roll back on him" (Proverbs 26:27).

Let's look at the good news within all of this—it's wonderful that we can choose the kind of harvest we reap! We can sow mercy and grace into others as our lifestyle and have an uninterrupted flow of it always coming back to us. We can always choose mercy over judgment, which is what our Heavenly Father always prefers (see James 2:13). Unrighteous judgment and condemnation hinder the glory of God, His manifest Presence, in our lives and in our churches. We don't have to continue to sabotage ourselves and short-circuit the glory of God.

THE COOKIE THIEF

by Valerie Cox[1]

A woman was waiting at an airport one night,
With several long hours before her flight.
She hunted for a book in the airport shops,
Bought a bag of cookies and found a place to drop.

She was engrossed in her book but happened to see,
That the man sitting beside her, as bold as could be,
Grabbed a cookie or two from the bag in between,
Which she tried to ignore to avoid a scene.

So she munched the cookies and watched the clock,
As the gutsy cookie thief diminished her stock.
She was getting more irritated as the minutes ticked by,
Thinking, "If I wasn't so nice, I would blacken his eye."

With each cookie she took, he took one, too,
When only one was left, she wondered what he'd do.

With a smile on his face, and a nervous laugh,
He took the last cookie and broke it in half.

He offered her half, as he ate the other,
She snatched it from him and thought, "Oooh, brother.
This guy has some nerve and he's also rude,
Why, he didn't even show any gratitude!"

She had never known when she had been so galled,
And sighed with relief when her flight was called.
She gathered her belongings and headed to the gate,
Refusing to look back at the thieving ingrate.

She boarded the plane and sank in her seat,
Then she sought her book, which was almost complete.
As she reached in her baggage, she gasped with surprise,
There was her bag of cookies, in front of her eyes.

If mine are here, she moaned in despair,
The others were his, and he tried to share.
Too late to apologize, she realized with grief,
That she was the rude one, the ingrate, the thief.

This poem so beautifully makes the point of one of life's greatest lessons. The woman judged her fellow traveler unrighteously in her heart and showed him no mercy! He gave her the benefit of the doubt and showed mercy and grace towards her. He could have gotten mad and said, "What are you doing eating my cookies?!" That's what she wanted to tell *him*! She didn't realize at the time that the verdict she was rendering against him was actually her own.

DAVID UNKNOWINGLY SENTENCED HIMSELF

Let's go back to the sins of King David when he committed adultery with Bathsheba and had her husband killed. For about a year David tried to cover his tracks and refused to deal with it. Was he thinking that with time it would all just go away? It is thought that during this time David wrote Psalms 32 and 38. When you read these psalms, you can see he is miserably lacking inner peace, and he is sick in body. The grace that he could be enjoying is not flowing into his life. He is refusing to listen to the Word, the Spirit, and his own conscience.

> *No greater punishment can any man have than to be left to have his own way.* **(AB)**

"Then the Lord sent Nathan to David" (2 Samuel 12:1). Nathan was coming to deliver God's righteous judgment, and it's a tribute to Nathan that he loved God enough to obey Him and loved David enough to try to help him out of his downward spiral. A true friend will not let you continue down a self-imposed path of destruction.

Nathan was a prophet, a friend, and one of David's most trusted advisors. Nathan told David about a rich man who had many lambs but who stole the one and only lamb of a poor man. What should be done to the rich man? King David flared up in anger and said the rich man must die! He didn't realize that the rich man he was judging was himself. He was the one who stole Uriah's only beloved wife, Bathsheba. "Then Nathan said to David, 'You are the man!'" (2 Samuel 12:7).

Now it's up to David. Will he admit his sin and have the truth about it? Will he humble himself and receive the grace that is ready to restore him and lift him up? David wrote Psalm 51 at this time, and he says to God in verse 6, "You desire truth in the inward parts." "So David said to Nathan, 'I have sinned against the Lord'" (2 Samuel 12:13). God is merciful and David was forgiven, but he still reaped some of the consequences that resulted from his bad actions.

GRACE AND TRUTH

"Grace and truth came through Jesus Christ" (John 1:17). They always come together. To the degree that you embrace and have truth in your life, to that degree you enjoy grace. Grace and truth flow together. You can't have one without the other. God has forever married grace and truth. Where Mr. Truth is welcomed and admitted, Mrs. Grace will always come along. This principle begins at salvation. If you won't embrace the truth that Jesus is Lord, you won't get the grace that saves and forgives. Only those who embrace the truth that they're lost will get the grace that brings them into salvation. If you won't humble yourself, well, there's no other answer, no other remedy, and no other way out. You must have the truth to receive the grace. The two are inseparable.

If you sweep the crumbs under the rug, you put yourself in a self-made prison. You can't go forward until you admit the truth and fully own it. A person in pride will never fully take the blame and own the truth for the wrong they've done. They will always try to deflect it and place it on someone else. Notice how early this evil tendency was birthed into the human race—Adam blamed his wife; then Adam blamed God for giving him the wife; Eve blamed the devil. Neither had the truth and said, "It was me. I was wrong."

If you choose to cling to the lie, you're choosing to remain in the devil's territory. He is the father of lies and does not abide in the truth (John 8:44). Buy the truth and fully own it (Proverbs 23:23). We never have to sell out to pride! We can always humble and use the key of truth, which will release us from our self-imposed prisons! Always remember this—in any area of my life in which I'm without enabling grace, I will have failure. I can never fail without rejecting the truth and believing the lie. This will always bring downfall, failure, a place of no grace. Grace and truth are inseparable; you can't have one without the other. When you humble and embrace the truth, you find that the grace of God automatically flows.

MERCY AND COMPASSION FOR OTHERS

I made my first missions trip in 1983 to the country of India. About six months before that trip, my wife discovered a lump in her breast. We both put our faith in God according to Mark 11:22-23, and I forgot about it. A month before my departure to India, my wife informed me that the lump was still there, and she was starting to get concerned about it. My response to her went something like this, "Chanler, where is your faith? It shouldn't take you five months to be healed of a lump, and why are you worrying about it if you're in faith?" As you can clearly see, no compassion, mercy, or understanding flowing out of my heart to her whatsoever.

About a week later, I noticed a red, ring-like spot on the inside of my right thigh. It soon spread to my stomach, down my legs, up my chest, and across my back, and it covered my arms as well. For some reason, it did not spread to my neck, face, or hands. I have never been assaulted before or since with such a painful, itching sensation. Whenever I removed my shirt, my skin would flake off and fall to the floor like dry snowflakes. I distinctly remember this thought coming to me: "Look at you! You can't go to India and minister to the sick. Those people will take one look at you and think that you've got leprosy. They'll turn and run in the opposite direction!" Of course, that thought was not from God.

I went to see a doctor, removed my shirt, and as my dry skin fell to the ground, he said, "Oh, boy, I've only seen this once before. It's called such-and-such. We don't know what causes it, and there is no known cure for it. The good news is that it takes six weeks to run its course and then it's gone." Well, that was not totally good news for me because it meant I would have this dreadful condition for the entire four weeks of my ministry in India. I knew that I had to get hold of God, but how little did I know that He wanted to get hold of me!

I came home from the doctor and told my wife, "No phone calls, no kids, no conversations, and no interruptions." I shut myself up in our guest bedroom for the next 24 hours with nothing but my Bible, a notepad, and a gallon of water. I alternated every 45 minutes between prayer and healing scriptures—a continual, non-stop cycle. At the end of that time of isolation, the Holy Spirit spoke something so clearly to my heart, and what He said was totally unexpected. He said, "Son, if you will humble yourself and go apologize to your wife for your proud, unmerciful, judgmental attitude toward her, your healing will begin to flow." Never have I ever been so glad to go to another person and tell her, "I am sorry!" Notice, too, what a merciful and wonderful thing it is

healing

when God offers us correction! It's His loving and gracious attempt to extract us out of our failure and restore us to a place of well-being again.

I woke up the next morning, after having apologized to my wife, and the first words out of my mouth were, "I know I am healed, and I have it now!" It was as if something tangible had been inserted down deep on the inside of me. Although all the physical symptoms were still there, "I knew that I knew that I knew" I was healed! Within two days' time, every bit of red, dry flesh had disappeared, and my skin was renewed like a baby's. Once I had humbled and bought the truth, the miracle-working grace of God flowed and did a quick work in my body. Instead of taking six weeks to heal, it took two days, and I was off to India, where I witnessed our compassionate Lord Jesus work miracle after miracle!

> *We don't really believe in grace until we minister it to others."* **(AB)**

Grace does not trample a person when he or she falls—rather, it says, "Let me help you up." It's never God who assigns me to put down another person and be their critic. Love has put us into the construction business—building others up—not the demolition business of tearing them down. Oh, and in case you're wondering: My wife's situation cleared up, too. No more lump, glory to God!

JACK AND JIM

Jesus sets the example for us in this important area of building people up. Do you remember how He flowed with the Father where judgments are concerned?

- "And He shall not judge by the sight of His eyes, nor decide by the hearing of His ears; but with righteousness He shall judge" (Isaiah 11:3-4).
- "Do not judge according to appearance, but judge with righteous judgment" (John 7:24).
- "I can of Myself do nothing. As I hear, I judge; and My judgment is righteous" (John 5:30).

> *It puts you in a place of dependency upon God, before you can render a righteous judgment. 'I don't know' and 'I refuse to judge for myself' is the only place that leads to righteous judgment. You will hear the voice of righteous judgment, as you refuse to move in your unrighteous judgment.*
> **(AB)**

Years ago, I heard this story about Jack and Jim, and it proves this point to the max! A church elder walked into a restaurant on a workday to have lunch. As he sat down, he looked across the room and saw another church member named Jim sitting across from a woman. He was holding her hands across the table, and the look of love was in his eyes, but the woman was not his wife!

The elder was stunned. What would Jim's wife think? This was going to devastate and destroy his family. The more he thought about it, the sicker he felt in his stomach.

"Well," he said to himself, "when he sees me, he is going to be completely embarrassed, and he should be!"

So the elder scooted his chair back and forth, thinking it would get Jim's attention—all to no avail. "This guy is so love-struck with this girl that nothing's going to get his attention," he thought. "I know what I'll do. I'll walk right by him to the restroom, and then he'll see me."

So the elder slowly strolled right past Jim's table, and it did absolutely nothing to break his fascination with this young lady. As he stood flabbergasted in the restroom, here's what he determined within himself that he would do: "I am going to confront him face to face for the sake of his family and our church!"

Boldly the elder walked up to Jim's table and let him have it. "Jim! I'm ashamed of you! What are you thinking? Have you lost your mind? What is this going to do to Martha? Don't you care at all about your kids? Plus, you've destroyed your testimony and tainted your reputation in the business world! What's gotten into you, Jim?"

Jim slowly pushed his chair back and stood to his feet. His face was turning a bright red, and he looked like he was using every bit of his self-control to restrain himself. Then, to the total shock of the elder, he said through gritted teeth, "I'm not Jim. I'm Jack—Jim's twin brother!"

Unless Jesus heard from the Father, He did not judge. That's why His judgments were always righteous. We, who are in Christ, must operate as the Man Christ operated! He always related to the Father in yielded submission. That's why He carried the glory, and the Spirit was upon His life "without measure!" I want to walk in the glory of God like that, too! Don't you?

CHAPTER 8
A BEAUTIFUL HEART

*Jesus is not God's abnormal man—we are
subnormal. Jesus is the Pattern Man.*

–Arthur Burt

"FOR I AM gentle and lowly in heart." Some versions
translate Jesus' words in Matthew 11:29 as *gentle
and humble in heart*. The root word for *humility* signi-
fies low-lying; not rising far from the ground; a bowed
heart. It paints a picture of not rising up, but bowing
low; the totally trusting heart of a laid-down lover of
God! Whenever we get glimpses of the throne of God in
the Book of Revelation, the 24 elders are always bowing
down and glorifying Him Who sits on the throne.

The Lord Jesus was sinless, yet He humbled Himself
as a continual lifestyle. Humility is not a demeaning,
condemning, kicking-yourself kind of lifestyle—we see
none of that in Jesus. A humble heart is not sin-conscious
or self-conscious because its very essence is selflessness.
A humble heart experiences total freedom from self!
With a humble heart, we lose all self-focus and become
totally occupied and enthralled with our God. There's

Someone inside you Who is gentle and humble. Clothe yourself with Him—His humility is yours to put on!

These lyrics from "Beautiful Heart," by Misty Edwards[1], describe Him well:

There is no shadow of turning in You

No rebellion or pride ...

You're gentle, You're meek, yet Your heart is strong ...

You don't hold a grudge or have a cynical eye,

Bitterness has no part of You ...

But humbly You live in perfect restraint ...

Jesus, You have a beautiful heart.

WHERE'S YOUR FOCUS?

We were made to live our lives connected to our God, just as a child lives in total dependence on his or her parent. We were meant to behold Him and everything about Him! "Our eyes look to the Lord our God" (Psalm 123:2). As we focus on and become totally occupied with God, we lose sight of ourselves—glorious freedom! Pride puts self where God should be, but as we look away from self and put our trusting gaze on God, everything about us falls into proper alignment.

Adam and Eve essentially had no self-consciousness until they lost their focus on God; when they fell, they fell into themselves and then became full of self-consciousness. Pride is tied to self-consciousness. Self-fixation is pride. Leaning upon the Lord in all things is humility.

Look to Jesus and lean on Him; humility is then in operation. Look to and lean upon yourself—pride automatically kicks in. Grace points you to Jesus; pride points you to yourself. Grace is the only area where self cannot take any credit. Grace safeguards the glory of God!

See all things that attempt to take your eyes off God as enemies, as seductions that need to be shunned. God—Most Beautiful One, Source of all Good, All Light, All Love—is basically being ignored and neglected daily. The focal point of man's interest and attention? Himself!

THE SPIDER AND THE CENTIPEDE

I don't remember where I heard this little story, but it clearly makes the point: The spider asked the centipede, "You have so many feet, how do you walk?" The centipede looked down and tried to figure it out and couldn't. The harder he tried, the more discouraged he got, and he effectively paralyzed himself—he could make no forward progress. After awhile, the sunlight broke through the clouds; and the centipede was so thrilled to see the light of the sun that he lost his concern over the order of his foot movement and began to run forward, making progress again.

If we become consumed with self-conscious introspection, always focused on ourselves, we lose sight of the One Who is the Source of all we need. We were never intended to live with our trust in ourselves. It's really not difficult to redirect our sight and live our lives with God as our focus. Instead of looking into the mirror to see ourselves, our heart's desire must be to look into the mirror to see our God. This is one of the easiest things in the world to do—simply whisper His Name throughout the day, "Father, Jesus, Holy Spirit." Be ever mindful that He is always present with you. Focus on Him, worship Him, and in all your ways acknowledge Him. Enjoy Him as you enter into more and more rest for your soul. You only have to love Him, worship Him, and flow in submission to Him. Free from "Me" with my eyes and my trust focused on Him, I can live with God-consciousness, free from all self-consciousness. The more I live my life focused on Him, the more my life will be saturated with His Presence, and the more my life will radiate His glory!

"LEARN FROM ME"—JESUS

Do you really, really believe that Jesus is to be our Teacher, our Master, and our Example in everything? Are you sure? If so, we can, "set [our] heart to understand, and to humble [ourselves] before our God" (Daniel 10:12).

Jesus instructs us, "Take My yoke upon you and learn from Me, for I am gentle and lowly in heart, and you will find rest for your souls. For My yoke is easy and My burden is light" (Matthew 11:29-30). Back in Bible days, entering a yoke meant entering into submission to another person. Jesus says His yoke is "easy." You'll like it and enjoy it; and it will fit you perfectly! Then, He calls His burden for you "light." A burden is a task and responsibility for you to bear. The all-wise God calls what He has for all of us "light and easy."

You were not meant to live life alone—independently—as if you were a god unto yourself. That way of living is hard and heavy. You were meant to live life yoked together with God—two lives living together as one—a life of intimate fellowship with Him. So let's carefully, meticulously learn from Him. Whatever we see in the Chief Son, Jesus, is what God has planned and ordained for all of His other sons and daughters. "Let this mind be in you which was also in Christ Jesus" (Philippians 2:5). Question: Will you? Will you let His way of thinking govern yours? How will you choose to think and live?

> We all have a purpose to fulfill in this life. How will we do it? The way He did it—Jesus is the Way—He is the pattern, and it will only work according to the pattern. **(AB)**

Well then, how did Jesus view this whole situation of living life to the glory of the Father? What was foremost on His heart and mind? What do we need to learn from Him? He "made Himself of no reputation" (Philippians 2:7). Jesus chose to live for His Father's reputation and not His own. That was a clear choice He had to make continually. Whose reputation do you care most about—yours or His? Pride will entice you to rise up and protect your reputation and image of yourself. Totally forget about all of that and be free from it. When I choose to make myself of no reputation, I've got no reputation to protect—wonderful freedom! I'm not living for the image that others try to project upon me. I'm living my life unto God. I don't care what people think of me. Jesus has set me free from all of that. My focus is Father's way, Father's heart, and Father's will. When that is my constant focus and desire, He conforms me into the image of His Son, Jesus.

"He humbled Himself and became obedient" (Philippians 2:8). Who did? The righteous, sinless Son of God. I want you to see that humbling yourself is a lifestyle and is not always connected with sin. Whose will are you choosing when you humble? His! Whose reputation do you care more about? His! Who are you exalting and putting first—yourself or God? Jesus "became obedient." Do you inwardly cringe and draw back when you hear the word *obedient*? Is that a dirty, unrighteous word to you? Jesus had a will that He always chose to lay down or humble, so that He could freely go with the way and the will of His Father.

- "Then I said, 'Behold, I come; in the scroll of the Book it is written of me. I delight to do Your will, O my God" (Psalm 40:7-8).

- "For I have come down from heaven, not to do My own will, but the will of Him who sent Me" (John 6:38).

So Jesus had His own will, and Father has His own will—two wills—which will will have its way? Jesus said, "I delight to do His!" It gave Him a high degree of gratification, extreme satisfaction, and great pleasure! You may ask, "Well, does choosing God's will give that to a person?" Yes, absolutely! The fall brainwashed us all to think that God's will is hard to swallow, unacceptable, and flawed; in reality it is "good and acceptable and perfect" (Romans 12:2).

"For it is God who works in you both to will and to do for His good pleasure" (Philippians 2:13). It does not say, "for His miserable, grievous, hard-to-bear load"! The devil will lie to you and tell you this will put you into bondage; instead, this is the way into continual rest and freedom. Do you remember "light and easy"? Jesus didn't see the Father's will as the ultimate, negative way to live. He didn't view it as a pleasure-less life of bondage. He saw it as the most blessed lifestyle and God's way to perfect completion. Jesus never questioned the Father's goodness—that's what makes it "easy" to do His will. Jesus' way of life was not abnormal. It's the only way that brings fulfillment to you and glory to God! So let the same heart and mind be in you that was in Christ Jesus: "I delight to do His will; I must be about My Father's business; I don't seek to do My own will, but the will of Him Who sent Me; and not My will, but Your will be done."

Is it a dirty, unrighteous thing to "humble yourself?" How about to "become obedient?" I think it's a shame that through books, paintings, and movies, we've been led to believe that Jesus lived a somber, almost sad life. The Bible tells us He was the most joyful man who has ever lived on planet earth! "You have loved righteousness and hated lawlessness; therefore God, Your God, has anointed You with the oil of gladness more than Your companions" (Hebrews 1:9). He happily loved what Father loved and hated what He hated; and it filled Him with extreme and perfect joy! Have you ever seen offered in churches or Bible schools a class on what we are to hate? Here, it specifically says that Jesus hated lawlessness. A lawless lifestyle is one that substitutes the will of self for the will of God. Jesus hated that; and in His own personal walk with the Father, He never chose it.

- "You who love the Lord, hate evil!" (Psalm 97:10).
- "The fear of the Lord is to hate evil; pride and arrogance and the evil way and the perverse mouth I hate" (Proverbs 8:13).
- "Hate evil, love good" (Amos 5:15).
- "Abhor what is evil. Cling to what is good" (Romans 12:9).

- "For what fellowship has righteousness with lawlessness?" (2 Corinthians 6:14).

Righteousness has its roots in God. Lawlessness has its roots in the devil. Those two can never be yoked together. So like Jesus, we hate the one and love the other; and to the degree that we let this govern our lifestyle, our experiencing of the joy of the Lord increases or decreases.

So where does all this lead, and is it all worth it? Well, besides having the glory of God manifesting in your life wherever you go and having your life glorify God, the highest honors from God are reserved for those who learn to live in the greatest humility. Notice this in the life of Jesus. He humbled Himself and became obedient; "therefore God also has highly exalted Him" (Philippians 2:9). His perfect honor and highest exaltation were directly connected to His perfect humility and submission. The highest honor in heaven goes to those with greatest humility on earth: "Before honor is humility" (Proverbs 15:33 and 18:12). "Therefore humble yourselves under the mighty hand of God, that He may exalt you in due time" (1 Peter 5:6).

TWO WILLS

Let's go back to the time when Peter and his fishing crew had been out all night working and came back with no fish. It's morning, and they are back on the shore cleaning their nets. Jesus appears and, of course, a large crowd gathers around Him. To make a little space for Himself, Jesus borrows one of Peter's boats so He can preach to the crowd on the shore. When He's finished, He tells Peter to go back out on the lake and throw out his nets for a haul of fish.

Two wills are involved here—the Lord's and Peter's. Will Peter humble and obey? Will He yield his will and go with the Lord's will in this situation? This is going to inconvenience him. He's just cleaned his nets and rolled them up after a hard night's work. Besides that, all fishermen know that you can't catch fish in the heat of the day. How will he look in the eyes of the other fishermen? What will this do to his reputation?

You can never live in the Presence if your greatest concern is how you look in the presence of men.
(AB)

Of the two wills involved, which will Peter choose? "Master, we have toiled all night and caught nothing; nevertheless at Your word I will let down the net" (Luke 5:5). Peter chose to humble, obey, and align his will with the Lord's. The result? They filled up both boats with fish to the point of sinking! The supernatural came on the scene, and God was glorified. When our wills are lined up with His, the things of heaven can then manifest upon the earth. Are you beginning to see that we were meant to live with our wills synchronized with

His? "Take My yoke upon you—it's a 24/7 yielding of your will—the lifestyle of a laid-down lover who worships Me in spirit and in truth."

Right from the beginning of His ministry, Jesus taught to everyone around Him this lifestyle of humble, yield, obey, and see the glory of God. In John 2 He's at the wedding feast in Cana and they have run out of wine. So Jesus tells those who were serving the guests, "Fill the waterpots with water" (John 2:7). I have read that these waterpots contained twenty to thirty gallons apiece and were used in the washing of feet. Next, "Draw some out now, and take it to the master of the feast" (John 2:8). Why would these servants want to take water from the foot washing pots and offer it to their boss? Not only are their reputations at stake, their jobs could be, too! Once again, we see the possible clash of two wills involved here—theirs and His. Whose will are they going to choose?

"I only do what I see the Father do," and "I must be about My Father's business." Jesus had lived His entire life according to that principle, and His mother knew it. So Mary tells the servants, "Whatever He says to you, do it" (John 2:5). They did as they were told, and the water they offered the master of the feast had been turned into wine. So here we see it again. As these servants humbled themselves and yielded their wills to His, they all saw the glory of God manifest around them! "This beginning of signs Jesus did in Cana of Galilee, and manifested His glory; and His disciples believed in Him" (John 2:11). Can you see that as we yield our wills to His, the gateway is opened for the glory of God to manifest? Power follows and flows through submission, and before all the people the Lord is glorified!

"IT'S THE FATHER WHO DWELLS WITHIN ME"—JESUS

We were never meant to live our lives alone. We were meant to live in dependency on and intimate fellowship with our God—two lives lived as one. All our problems start when, like sheep, we turn astray, deciding to go our own way (Isaiah 53:6). "He who says he abides in Him ought himself also to walk just as He walked" (1 John 2:6).

> *Jesus is the Pattern Man, and if we truly desire to follow and live like Him, it will only work according to pattern. The man in Christ must operate as the Man, Christ, operated.* **(AB)**

Most people mistakenly believe that Jesus lived a lifestyle that was off limits to everyone else. They falsely think that it's impossible for anyone to walk with the Father like Jesus did. But notice carefully what Jesus said about His walk with Father God: "The words that I speak to you I do not speak on My own authority;

but the Father who dwells in Me does the works" (John 14:10).

All that Jesus ever did, He never did. **(AB)**

Jesus did what He did by the power of Another! It was the Father dwelling in Him Who did the works and manifested His glory. We have the same Greater One living in us, and He wants to reveal His power, character, and glory through us as He did through His Pattern Son, Jesus. Jesus is the First Born of the new creation nation of God. Jesus is the prototype—the model—the Head of God's new breed. If we're going to "walk just as He walked," we're going to have to learn of Him and do it His way. He *is* the Way!

Jesus was the only one on earth Who never lived independently from the Father. He constantly cooperated with the Father, yielding to the Father's will and promptings. Jesus yielded His life so completely to the Father that He became the Father's perfect expression to the earth. As He lived totally depending upon His Father God, He enjoyed perfect completion, sufficiency, and grace. Wait, grace? Saving grace? No, Jesus was without sin—He never needed saving grace—but He did need *enabling* grace. Grace enabled Jesus to be all that He was and to do all that He did.

- "And the Child grew and became strong in spirit, filled with wisdom; and the grace of God was upon Him" (Luke 2:40).

- "And we beheld His glory, the glory as of the only begotten of the Father, full of grace and truth" (John 1:14).

Jesus was always full of grace because He always walked in full humility toward the Father. When you choose to humble and go God's way, His grace flows automatically; His enabling grace is free to flow, and His glory is displayed for all to see! Grace is the enabling power of God that conforms you to Christ's character and performs His same works of power through you. A true understanding of grace will keep us in a position of constant humility and dependence as we look in faith to "the God of all grace" (1 Peter 5:10).

"OF MY OWN SELF? NOTHING!"—JESUS

Jesus had a will that He always chose to submit to the Father. He had a "self" that always chose to humble and bow. Jesus never operated out of self. Notice in the scriptures below how He always allowed the Father to originate and take the lead in everything.

- "The Son can do nothing of Himself, but what He sees the Father do" (John 5:19).

- "I can of Myself do nothing. As I hear, I judge" (John 5:30).

- "I do nothing of Myself; but as My Father taught Me, I speak these things" (John 8:28).

- "The Father who dwells in Me does the works"
  (John 14:10).

So instead of Jesus moving independently and of His own accord, He simply relied upon the Father for what to say, what to do, and how to judge and decide. Consequently, Father was always free to say and do His own glorious works through His Son. Jesus' will never collided or disagreed with His Father's, so Jesus never experienced a power failure or character glitch. Because He always gave a full measure of submission to the Father, the Spirit was always upon Jesus' life "without measure" (see John 3:34). The measure in which we are currently flowing and living in the Spirit is directly related to the measure in which we are yielding to and relying upon Him. Jesus lived a 100 percent yielded lifestyle, and this is for you, too! God will be in you what He was in Christ, and God will do through you what He did through Christ, if you will trust and yield yourself to Him. Let's face it, the Bible was not given to us just to be memorized and studied, but to be materialized in us with beautiful character and magnificent power! "He who believes in Me, the works that I do he will do also; and greater works than these will he do, because I go to My Father" (John 14:12).

OUR GLORIOUS LIFESTYLE

We are all called to walk in the Spirit. To live in the Spirit is to be guided by another Person from within. Under the Old Covenant, God was outside the people; He gave a Law, they studied it and tried to do it. Under the New Covenant, God leads and empowers us from within as we trust and lean on Him. We submit to the control of the Holy Spirit; and in complete dependence upon Him, we conduct ourselves by His guidance, impulses, and power. He's a Person Who's always with us, sharing every experience we encounter day and night. He's not just in the hills, in the clouds, beyond the stars and sky. He's not just at the meetings on Sundays and on Wednesday nights.

To be spiritual is to live your everyday life together with Jesus. Go about your day with Him as your Guide, Counselor, Friend, and Helper in everything you do. Do not try to live by your own natural strength or wisdom like all other religions do—rather, live by relying on the Greater One, the All-Wise One, Who lives inside of you. Are you willing to depend upon Him? Are you willing to release the control of your "self" to the Master? The full, enabling grace of God kicks into action in your life when you do! Grace begins to flow when human ability ends. God then, "is able to do exceedingly abundantly above all that we ask or think, according to the power that works in us" (Ephesians 3:20).

"To Him be glory in the church" (Ephesians 3:21). Of course! His is the power and the glory forever, amen! Too often we don't bow to God. We make our own decisions and set our own course, never thinking that we should consult the Lord first. Relying on ourselves—leaning to our own understanding—we move independently and bring forth rotten fruit. Since Jesus is our All-Wise, All-Sufficient Lord, why would we ever think of acting independently? Jesus never operated out of "self." "Self" was never His starting point. He constantly cooperated with the Father, yielding to the Father's direction.

The Spirit of God flows through you also when you humble, bow, and yield to Him. Follow His promptings, urges, inner checks—pay attention to the Christ within you. Jesus wants the right of action that will reveal Himself through you to the world around you. He wants to be glorified in your life. The impulses of your being can be in complete harmony with His. Jesus demonstrated man's capacity to reveal God to the earth. God lives in you today to transmit His character, power, and glory—now we are the body of Christ on the earth. God's intention is that the Christian should be a revelation of Christ. We are inhabited by the glorified Christ, and God placed us in this world to demonstrate Christ to the glory of the Father. Let's allow God to be as free to manifest Himself through us as He did through Christ! What an awesome and priceless privilege!

The Giver of all gifts, Jesus Christ, is resident within every born-again believer and can manifest in any way, at any time, if I am sensitive and learn to yield to His promptings. **(AB)**

We mistakenly believe we can do it ourselves — we believe we can make our own decisions, our own judgments, set our own course in life and somehow God will bless it. We rely on our own self-sufficiency and take the initiative away from God, setting ourselves in the place of God. But we were created to live in total dependence to God, and such a dependence begets the only real independence; for then we face life not in our own strength but in God's, and thus we experience His victory! **(AB)**

We were meant to live by listening to the voice of God — by every word that proceeds out of the mouth of God. There is simplicity in walking in humility — it is not rocket science! The only barrier is my stubborn will when it refuses to bow to the promptings of the Holy Spirit. The human heart needs to be Christ-ruled. Self-rule needs to bow out with all its anarchy of independence. My way needs to hit the highway if it doesn't coincide with His way. **(AB)**

The Master works with us to finely tune our lives to become carriers of His Presence. The Presence is the birthright of each believer when we are flowing as one with the Spirit of Christ, our Head. I believe this is what will constitute the next move of God on the earth—a ministry of His Presence.
(AB)

CHAPTER 9
ORIGINATIONS ARE ALL IMPORTANT

*The "best" of your flesh is actually
the worst of your flesh.*

–Arthur Burt

"FOR I KNOW that in me (that is, in my flesh) nothing good dwells" (Romans 7:18). This is a fact that the Apostle Paul was absolutely certain about; and yet, I wonder how many Christians have ever realized what he's referring to. Our "flesh" could be described as anything that originates from our natural selves: all human abilities, attainments, or works that are not rooted in and flowing out of us from God. Whatever we do without trusting and relying upon God is of the flesh. If "nothing good" dwells in my flesh, then, whatever comes forth from my flesh is no good! Anything I do that does not come forth from God's Spirit is nothing. When I move in the flesh, I pave the way to my own failure. Only decay, ruin, and collapse can ever come out of the flesh—flesh always fathers failure. "It is the Spirit Who gives life; the flesh profits nothing" (John 6:63).

Here's where it gets tricky, and we get tripped up.

None of us puts confidence in the "worst" of our flesh—lust, deceit, anger, drunkenness, envy, strife, or selfishness. No! No! Absolutely not! But we have a tendency to put confidence in the "best" of our flesh; and, in so doing, we disconnect our faith and reliance upon God and end up depending upon ourselves! Self-righteous works of the flesh always appear "good," but flesh remains flesh no matter how "good" it appears. The thing of utmost importance is the source—did it originate from God? Anything originating from self and done in natural ability is spiritually useless and unprofitable. Self can perform things that look good without any connection to or reliance upon the Holy Spirit.

Any good that originates with me and is done by my own wisdom and effort will always try to puff up self. It will be self-originated, self-performed, self-righteous, and all done to the glory of self. However "good" the plans and deeds of the flesh appear to be, "I" is always lurking in the background. Self always tries to take the lead and get the Spirit to follow. If I am the source, I will inevitably ascribe the glory to myself. A man's own fleshly efforts glorify the man; "Look at what I've done!" When we rely on the Spirit, He always glorifies Jesus; "Look at what the Lord has done!" Flesh always put self where God should be. So it's easy to see that when we rely on and operate in the flesh, we produce nothing of worth, and God is not glorified.

WHERE IS YOUR CONFIDENCE?

"We should not trust in ourselves but in God who raises the dead" (2 Corinthians 1:9). We were never meant to live trusting in ourselves, but to live by continually leaning upon the chest of our All-Sufficient Father God. Let's take a quick inventory. Who or what are you leaning on? Your will power? Your money? Your credentials? Your degrees? Your influence? Your contacts? Your good looks? Your personality? Yourself?

If I trust in myself to help and empower myself, I cancel out the help of Christ. I don't have to lean on my own ability, but I can lean on God's limitless ability. Faith is occupied with the Lord and pays no attention to itself at all. I totally lean upon my Father God, and I know that He will never let me down. My eyes are on Him. My confidence is in Him. I know that it's never by my might or my power, but it's always by His Spirit. I know that as I trust in Him, His power will work in me and do excessively more than the situation even requires! To Him be all the glory! (See Ephesians 3:20-21.)

NO CONFIDENCE IN THE FLESH

"For we are the circumcision, who worship God in the Spirit, rejoice in Christ Jesus, and have no confidence in the flesh" (Philippians 3:3). Paul gives us here, in nutshell form, the way we are all meant to serve and conduct ourselves as citizens of the kingdom of God. Let's break this down and see what he's saying.

I love to sing with all my heart to God, but when Paul says we "worship God in the Spirit," he's not speaking of worshiping God in song but about how we serve and follow God in the power of the Holy Spirit. We serve by His directings and by His power—He's the Source and the empowerment behind everything we do in the kingdom. To be effective, we must realize that we must always rely upon "a demonstration of the Spirit and of [His] power" (see 1 Corinthians 2:4-5). So Christ then becomes the One Who is displaying His wisdom, His fruit, His power, and His glory in our midst, and we are always rejoicing and boasting in Christ alone! We are always boasting, but not in ourselves, our flesh, or in any human attainment. Our glory is in Christ alone.

So many times in my life I have entered into a crucial situation not having any idea or clue what to do. I have said to the Lord, "Jesus, think through me, speak through me, and flow through me. I am totally trusting and relying upon You." Time after time, He has worked out those situations so smoothly, so amazingly, that I have said to Him over and over, "Oh Wonderful Jesus, glory be to Your Name forever!" So we make Christ Jesus the only One in Whom we boast.

"And have no confidence in the flesh." Paul then goes on to say that if anyone had fleshly things to confide in, he certainly did! Notice what he lists as fleshly attributes in Philippians 3:5-6—his race and family pedigree, his studies and scholastic attainments, his religious zeal and dedication, and his reputation of being a strict keeper of the law—in other words, the "best" of his flesh. The attributes and attainments of the flesh are no substitute for the power and fruit of the Holy Spirit.

I am a learner. I love to study, and I place a high value on the right kind of education, but I don't place my confidence and reliance upon those things. I also realize that if lean on anything other than Jesus, that's where I'm placing confidence in my flesh!

> *By dwelling in the shadows of our own fleshly attributes, we shut out the glorious light of Jesus that could be filling and spilling out from our souls. When we put our trust in anything besides God, we set up a king, an idol, to which we give God's glory away. When we trust in ourselves, we are sucking the breast of our own self-sufficiency— not the breast of Christ, our El Shaddai, and so Christ becomes a dry nurse to us—we forfeit His all-sufficiency.* **(AB)**

OUR SUFFICIENCY? GOD!

"Not that we are sufficient of ourselves to think of anything as being from ourselves, but our sufficiency is from God" (2 Corinthians 3:5). So this is something that we can settle once and for all—anything we depend upon other than God is a false idol and will always prove insufficient. We know that we are not self-sufficient. All of our adequacy, power, abilities and resources come from God. He is our sufficiency. We know that our flesh will always try to squeeze out and usurp the authority of the Holy Spirit so that none of His abilities can flow through us; but that is no longer permissible. We must realize that all our sufficiency comes from God and not from ourselves. He is our sufficiency. We can and must rely on Him, and in Him we have everything we need!

WIGGLESWORTH, A SIMPLE MAN

Many times in my conversations with Arthur Burt, I have asked him about his time spent with Smith Wigglesworth. Smith was known as a man who had audacious faith in his God. He saw the dead raised, limbs restored, the blind receive sight, etc. His family removed him from school in the second grade so that he could work in the fields and help the family survive financially. He was almost totally deprived of an education and could barely read and write. So here we have a man who is the total opposite of the highly educated Apostle Paul. Paul had many areas in which he could trust in his flesh, and Smith had basically none.

> *Smith Wigglesworth? One of the simplest people I ever met. I lived for a season with this ordinary*

man that everybody thinks was extra-ordinary. My wife washed his clothes. My friend did his finances. He left school at the age of eight. In one letter he wrote, he spelled Holy Spirit five different ways. But he was a man of the Spirit; and, therefore, wonderfully blessed of God in his ordinary-ness. **(AB)**

Wigglesworth said of himself, "I am here before you as one of the biggest conundrums in the world. There never was a weaker man on the platform. Language? None. Inability? Full of it. All natural things in my life point exactly opposite to me being able to stand on the platform and preach the gospel."[1]

Arthur has told me that when Smith began a sermon by reading from the Bible, his speech was so slow and faltering that it was pitifully painful for all the listeners. Then suddenly, like a rocket launching from its platform, he would tap in and flow with the Spirit. When he tapped into the Spirit, it was remarkable. Everyone in the building could notice the difference. Wigglesworth said, "I see everything a failure except that which is done in the Spirit. But as you live in the Spirit, you move, act, eat, drink, and do everything to the glory of God."[2]

Wigglesworth was not a great man—he had a great God, and he learned how to flow with Him. **(AB)**

Take encouragement, everyone! We all have the same great God, and we can learn how to flow with Him, too!

GETTING BACK TO JESUS

Of Jesus, Wigglesworth said, "I find that all my Lord did, He said that He did not do it, but that another in Him did the work. What a holy submission! He was just an instrument for the glory of God.... When my love is so deepened in God that I only move for the glory of God, that I only seek the glory of God, then the gifts can be made manifest. God wants to be manifested and to manifest His glory to humble spirits."[3] His "doing nothing" led to the Father being able to do everything through Jesus. Jesus came to show us Another—His Father! We, too, have come to show the world Another—our magnificent Lord Jesus! When we fully yield, we open the door for Him to fully flow through us and manifest Himself to the world around us. This is the lifestyle of humility—a moment-by-moment yielding to the King Who lives within us.

God's plan is for Christ to relive His life in and through us, enabling us to be and do what in our own strength we could never be or do! God's plan is that the Holy Spirit lives the life of Christ in us. To walk in the Spirit and be led by the Spirit, we have to be continually conscious of His Presence in us, knowing that because

He resides in us, we have everything we need for this life in the Spirit.

Our life is Christ living out His life from within our life. As we rely upon the Spirit within, He will initiate, direct, and empower us from the inside out. We now live a simple life of faith in total dependence upon the Holy Spirit. Remember, it's light and easy! (See Matthew 11:30.) We simply live by a confidence in and an allegiance and loyalty to the Son of God within. We are His body, His temple on the earth, and His Spirit actually dwells in us. He has come to live His life and display His glory through us. We live now by the Life of Another, not by our own life. Faith in Christ is the element by which I now live, as opposed to faith in myself and living by the flesh. Faith realizes that anything rooted in the flesh is helpless, weak, and ineffective, so it depends totally upon God and His ability. Faith relies on God— His leading, His power, His wisdom, His promptings; and, in total dependence, it yields and flows with Him. Faith counts on God with absolute dependence and perfect confidence.

Do you realize that God has made you a carrier of His Presence, and He wants to manifest his glory through you? What would your life look like free from all inhibitions—with nothing holding you back? You could flow freely with God anywhere—having the right words, praying with His power, and releasing His love to everyone you meet. You would be a free-flowing spirit, ministering the glory, power, and Presence of Another. What a worthy goal to pursue with all of our hearts for the rest of our lives!

So teach us, Lord, to trust and yield to the Holy Spirit and to trust and yield—at no time—to the way of the flesh. We purpose to live and flow out of our attachment to Christ. We know that Christ in us is our sure hope of glory! (Colossians 1:27).

CHAPTER 10
DEMONSTRATIONS

I said, "God is real!" because of a demonstration!
                                        –Arthur Burt

FROM THE UNSEEN TO THE SEEN

W E KNOW THAT the Bible testifies that David was a man after God's own heart. In other words, David wanted what God wanted, and for all the right reasons! David knew that God is omnipresent, that is, present everywhere at all times. "Where can I go from Your Spirit? Or where can I flee from Your presence?" (Psalm 139:7). He is always with us whether we feel or sense His presence. We live by faith in that fact, and it has nothing to do with our feelings. I have experienced some great breakthroughs when I had no feelings or sense of His power or Presence at all. We don't live or base our faith in God by what we feel or see. Yet, there is a very real reality of God's manifest Presence. David also said, "So I have looked for You in the sanctuary to see Your power and Your glory" (Psalm 63:2). Was David wrong to desire this? Was this a godly desire that burned within his heart?

Apostle Paul was certainly a strong teacher of faith: "The just shall live by faith" (Romans 1:17); "The word of faith which we preach" (Romans 10:8); "For we walk by faith, not by sight" (2 Corinthians 5:7). But Paul was also a very strong advocate of physical demonstrations of God's power and physical manifestations of His Spirit. "And my speech and my preaching were not with persuasive words of human wisdom, but in demonstration of the Spirit and of power, that your faith should not be in the wisdom of men but in the power of God" (1 Corinthians 2:4-5).

Do you believe that Paul was inspired of God and that his desire for these people was also God's desire? Of course. Well then, God wanted these people to be ushered into His kingdom by seeing a demonstration of His power and a manifestation of His Spirit. He wanted these new believers to have a foundational faith in the power of God!

SHE WAS BORN BLIND

Now that's where life began for me at age 15. I didn't know a thing. I'd never been to church, never been to Sunday school. I was an absolute heathen. But I saw this girl, she'd be about 20. She had been born blind. Suddenly she was jumping up and down hysterically shouting, 'Oh, I can see! I can see!' And that one thing was a demonstration that began God dealing with this man—me. I said, 'God is real!' because of a demonstration! **(AB)**

We are coming back to the realization that God has always desired a "demonstration." Not to convince us that He is real and with us—to convince *others!*

Jesus walked in a steady stream of demonstrations of Spirit and power. His life seemed to be a walking manifestation of the glory of God! "Men of Israel, hear these words: Jesus of Nazareth, a Man attested by God to you by miracles, wonders, and signs which God did through Him" (Acts 2:22). Notice that God did the works through Jesus and validated Him and His message by demonstrations. God has always desired to confirm the Word of both Jesus and His followers: "God also bearing witness both with signs and wonders, with various miracles, and gifts of the Holy Spirit" (Hebrews 2:4).

THIS IS FOR YOU!

"He who says he abides in Him ought himself also to walk just as He walked" (1 John 2:6). If you're a born-again follower of Jesus, then you abide in Him and He abides in you. What an exciting lifestyle—to walk as He walked! Remember, it's not by our own ability or qualifications, it's by His Spirit. We live this life by totally relying upon Christ within us. We are His representatives on the earth, showing the world His beautiful heart and character. God also wants to work through us and show the world His power and glory, just like He did through the physical body of Jesus when He walked the earth. Now we are the Body of Christ upon the earth, and God wants the world to see the character and power of Jesus through our lives. Whatever you see in Jesus is God's way and purpose for you! That's your destiny!

In Jesus' walk on the earth, He displayed that beautiful heart of humility. He was gentle and full of compassion. As we rely upon Christ within us, we can display that beautiful character, too. But did He not also walk in the miraculous? That's His calling for us as well—to walk as He walked! We are not called to a life of passive inactivity. Jesus came and got fully involved with a dirty, sick, sinful world. He planted Himself right in the middle of all its chaos. That's our calling too—to be free-flowing channels of God's power, love, and mercy to a world that God so dearly loves and cherishes. The lives of so many Christians resemble those of professional students who never leave college to go out into the world to put into practice what they've learned in class. Don't be a person who enjoys education more than experiencing and walking in what you've learned. God desires demonstration!

"And there are also many other things that Jesus did, which if they were written one by one, I suppose that even the world itself could not contain the books that would be written. Amen" (John 21:25). Do you grasp the significance of what John said there? If the testimonies of every life that was miraculously affected by Jesus were recorded, the world would have trouble containing all the books! And that was all accomplished in only three and a half years of ministry through one Person! How much more can God do today through the many-personed Body of Christ?

God has marked us all out to become like the pattern we see in His Son—to live the same kind of life He did. God put His Spirit in you for a great purpose! His ministry is to always glorify Jesus. That's what He's always at work in you to do; to speak Jesus' words, develop Jesus' character, produce Jesus' works of power, and always/only to glorify Jesus through you. He's in you to enable you to walk as Jesus walked.

Let's get back to how Jesus walked (1 John 2:6). When we consider the magnitude and the frequency of the demonstrations that accompanied and surrounded His lifestyle, how could we possibly settle for a once-in-a-lifetime demonstration? Or once a year? Or even once a month?

WIND AND FIRE

"Now when the Day of Pentecost had fully come, they were all with one accord in one place. And suddenly there came a sound from heaven, as of a rushing mighty wind, and it filled the whole house where they were sitting. Then there appeared to them divided tongues, as of fire, and one sat upon each of them" (Acts 2:1-3). The Holy Spirit manifested and came like a hurricane! Then, as they looked at one another, each of them had a manifestation of fire upon his or her head! Talk about demonstrations! Were they expecting that? Were they living by their flesh, being led by their feelings? No! They were simply following His orders—all of them in submission to Jesus, their Head. They were all in one heart, in one accord with the Lord, and they had gathered in the place of His choosing.

"And when this sound occurred, the multitude came together" (Acts 2:6). On the Day of Pentecost the glory of God manifested as a sound, and people were drawn to it. After the crowd was gathered, Peter preached the gospel to them, and 3,000 people were added to the kingdom that day. The manifestation of the glory of God is for the expansion of the kingdom of God!

GOD'S GLORY IN FRANCE

The first time I went to France, I took a team of eight with me from my local church. We went to help and encourage an American missionary friend who had faithfully pastored there for five years. His church had 30 converts, which at that time was an average-sized church in France. The first night, everyone was very excited and wholeheartedly sang and worshiped the Lord. Toward the end of that praise and worship service, the Lord clearly showed me that He wanted us to take that same wholehearted praise out on the streets. I gulped, bowed my heart to the Lord, and told the pastor we were willing to do that. He was thrilled! He said, "We'll start tomorrow, and I know the perfect crossroads where we can set up!"

If you've been to France, you know the streets are narrow and the buildings are usually about three stories high and built close to the streets. We set up at a crossroads, in the middle of the day, where there was a lot of foot traffic. On my team I had two guitar players, some good singers, and one college-aged woman who performed beautiful spiritual dances to the Lord. None of them had ever done anything quite like this before. I told them to get in their own bubble with God, shut out the physical world, and by faith express all their love and gratitude to the Lord.

So the musicians played, the singers sang, and the

dancer danced. After about thirty minutes we were soaking in the wonderful manifest presence of God! I opened my eyes, and to my surprise here's what I saw: We were surrounded by French people. You should have seen their faces! They were enthralled, and many of them had tears streaming down their faces. Women were on their balconies and hanging out their windows listening and coming under the influence of His Presence!

I told my team, "Okay, everybody, go to those you are drawn to and lead them to the Lord." We had 28 born again that day. The pastor could hardly believe it! He had labored faithfully for five years and gathered 30. His church had almost doubled in an hour. What did we attribute that to? The Presence of God had saturated and enveloped those people. He had drawn them to Jesus. "But You are holy, Who inhabit the praises of Israel" (Psalm 22:3). That day the Lord inhabited our praises in France!

MUSTANG GLORY

Jesus taught us always to pray and never to stop. I believe prayer is an avenue that can help bring the things from the unseen realm of God into the seen realm here on earth. One of the pillars of our local church is to always keep everything bathed in regular prayer, so we have several weekly prayer meetings for this purpose. One night a group of us had prayed for about seven hours.

It had been a particularly "dry" night of prayer, but we know that "the eyes of the Lord are on the righteous, and His ears are open to their prayers" (1 Peter 3:12). We know by faith in His Word that He hears and answers apart from our feelings.

I gathered the group in a circle at about 2 a.m. and said, "Before we go home, let's just praise and thank God with all of our hearts for a few minutes." Well, for about ten minutes everyone did just that and, suddenly, one of the most powerful manifestations of God's presence I've ever felt exploded in the middle of our circle! It affected every one of us in that circle. A sixteen-year-old girl dropped to her knees and cried, out, "It's Jesus! Oh, it's Jesus!" I looked to my left and the people looked like they were being blown around by the wind of a hurricane. I looked across from me and one of our elders, who is a scientist, was looking up through the ceiling. Myself? I felt like I was one step away from moving out of the physical realm and literally stepping into the unseen realm of the Spirit. I mean disappearing out of the physical! For some reason I couldn't get there. All of this continued to manifest for 45 minutes. Then it lifted and ended as suddenly as it had begun.

The scientific elder sat us all down and described to us what he had seen. Keep in mind that his way of thinking was very logical and analytical. Here's what he told us: "As we all began to praise Him, I suddenly saw shafts of light come out of everyone's stomach area.

These shafts all converged in the middle of the circle and then went up straight through the ceiling as one shaft of light. As we continued to praise, the shaft continued ceaselessly up, up, up. I was fascinated! All of sudden, as our shaft of praise continued to go up, a much larger shaft of light came down, enveloping our shaft of praise. When it hit the floor in the middle of the circle, that's when our young sister cried out, 'It's Jesus!'" Well to say the least, we all left that prayer meeting saturated, fascinated, and in awe. But little did I know that things were about to get really interesting.

I had a 1966 Mustang at the time, and one of the single guys needed a ride home. I dropped him off at his apartment, which was close to the downtown area, at about 4 a.m. As soon as he got inside, it began to pour. As I was driving in this downpour, a motorcycle pulled up right beside me, and the driver made motions at me with his hand. My thoughts went like this, "Is he making an obscene gesture? Does he want to fight me?" And I quoted to myself, "God has not given me a spirit of fear, but of power, love, and a sound mind!" Keep in mind that it was 4 a.m., pouring rain, and nobody else was on the road. I sped up, and he sped up. I slowed down, and he slowed down. I could not shake him.

I knew we were coming up to a traffic light two blocks from my house, and I decided to trust God's Spirit inside me and confront this head on. At the red light, I rolled down my window and said, "Hey, what's up?"

He said, "I've been playing cards and drinking beer. What's up with you? Do you want to go get a beer?"

I said, "I've been in a prayer meeting all night praying for you and everyone else in the city of Boulder, and, no, I don't want to get a beer. I live two blocks up the street. Do you want to follow me home and hear about it?"

He nodded and followed me home on his motorcycle. I invited him into my pitch-black house, where my wife and girls were safely asleep, turned on the light over the dining room table, and, as he sat silently across from me, I gave him the whole plan of redemption from Genesis to the resurrection. After 45 minutes of my nonstop talking, I asked him, "Well, what about it? Are you ready to bow your knee to Jesus and make Him your Lord?"

This is all he said, "No, sir, but I will consider carefully everything you've said."

I walked him to the door with his helmet in his hand and told him, "If you ever need to talk to me, you know where I live." He fired up his motorcycle and rode off into the darkness. I closed the door, sat down in the darkness of my house, and asked myself, "What just happened? And how in the world did that happen?" You know what I think? In the darkness of that rainstorm, the light of God's glory filled my little Mustang. Mustang glory!

THE GLORY OF GOD IN MEXICO

Keep in mind that experiences with the glory of God are happening all over the world. I want to share with you a few recent testimonies that personal friends of mine have told me.

Aaron and Karrie Kolb have been faithful missionaries to Mexico for 36 years. I have known Aaron for 26 years. He is a man with a proven reputation—a man of truth and integrity. Below are two of Aaron's stories, in his own words.

TOLUCA, MEXICO: "I was invited to a precious church in Toluca, Mexico. Pastor Reynoldo and I have been friends for 30 years. This Saturday night as I was ministering on the Song of Solomon about the kisses of our King, we got a big kiss from the Lord's presence.

"Suddenly you could sense a great shift in the spiritual atmosphere. It got really thick, and the ministry of the Holy Spirit just broke out. All over the church people began to cry, shake, and fall to their knees. Many testified that in that powerful presence of God they were healed.

"Then an amazing thing happened. The place literally shook. It shook right at the moment when the Holy Spirit's presence flooded that place. It lasted for about ten to fifteen seconds, and we all thought it was just a normal earthquake.

"To everyone's big surprise, when we left the meeting

we asked the neighbors and those outside about the earthquake. They all said, "No, there was no earthquake that evening." That's when we all realized it was just our church building that shook that night! We had Acts 4:31 happen to us in Toluca!"

Is it wrong to expect this? Notice what the early church prayed: "'Now, Lord, look on their threats, and grant to Your servants that with all boldness they may speak Your word, by stretching out Your hand to heal, and that signs and wonders may be done through the name of Your holy Servant Jesus.' And when they had prayed, the place where they were assembled together was shaken; and they were all filled with the Holy Spirit, and they spoke the word of God with boldness" (Acts 4:29-31). The original church prayed for healings, signs, and wonders to be done. If that's something we shouldn't pray, as some teach today, why didn't God or one of the apostles correct it? Instead of telling them they were wrong, God confirmed their prayer with a sign and filled them all with Holy Ghost boldness!

We know that Jesus was raised from the dead by the glory of the Father (see Romans 6:4) and that the raising of the dead was part of the gospel commission that was given to those early disciples (see Matthew 10:7-8). Before Jesus raised Lazarus from the dead He told Martha, "Did I not say to you that if you would believe, you would see the glory of God?" (John 11:40). Here are two tremendous things revealed to us from the lips of

Jesus. First, every time someone is raised, the glory of God is manifested. Second, He actually encourages us to believe in order to "see the glory of God"! He is actually telling us what He wants us to believe for!

Believe for an atmosphere filled with the glory of God that enables people to experience and have a living encounter with the Lord of Glory. Signs always point to Him, and their purpose is to help people come under His Lordship. Pray and believe for this.

MEXICO CITY, MEXICO: "This night of ministry was in a home group where hungry souls would come and receive the Word of God. As I was finishing a message on the authority we have in Jesus' Name, a sister named Gloria walked into the back of the room carrying her 8-year-old daughter in her arms. I was inviting anyone that needed prayer to come to the front. As Gloria came forward with her daughter in her arms, I could see her face was covered with tears.

"As I looked at her daughter with her face covered with a blanket, I thought she had been sick and needed healing. Since I had just preached on the power of Jesus' Name, I sensed great faith in my heart and laid hands on her daughter. Well, to me it seemed that her daughter just woke up from a nap. She looked up at her mom and said in Spanish, '*Todo bien, Mama,*' which means, 'All is well, Mom.' Then she stood up and smiled. Gloria fell to her knees, raised her hands, and began to loudly praise God. All the others in the place began to do the same. Because everyone was shouting, yelling, crying, and praising so loudly I knew something powerful had just happened.

"I pulled my friend Ricardo close to me and asked, '¿Qué está pasando, Ricardo?' ('What's happening, Ricardo?') What he told me shook me.

"'Pastor Aaron, you didn't know this, but Gloria's daughter drowned in a swimming pool during her class an hour ago. She was dead, Pastor, and Jesus just raised her from the dead!'

"When Ricardo told me this, I began to join with everyone else, jumping and shouting and praising God! Thank you, Jesus!

"Immediately after this miracle, Gloria's husband, Fabio, gave his heart to Jesus and has been faithfully serving Him ever since."

HE'S THE LIVING GOD

God wants people to know Who He is and what He's really like. So remember, His glory is His manifest presence—it's the goodness of God being revealed and released upon a person, place, or situation. The glory of God is all that He is, made visible for all to see—the tangible manifestation of God. When God fills the physical realm with what is always in His spiritual realm, that's His glory! God's not dead—He's alive! He's not a book or a doctrine—He's the Living God! He has not retired and pulled the plug on His power—He is the actively employed Almighty God!

NORTHERN INDIA INVADED BY THE GLORY OF GOD

My long-time friends Mark and Sharmila Anderson are evangelists who minister all over the world, but particularly in Sharmila's home country of India. I have known Mark since 1986 (he has written an excellent book—Humility, The Hidden Key to Walking in Signs and Wonders). I have asked them to write about some of their recent experiences in Northern India:

"In Northern India, only one percent of the people are Christian. These areas have been known for severe persecution of Christians (some have been beaten to death by militant Hindus). You can understand why in many towns there are no churches at all.

"Often as we worship Jesus the Creator, His glorious presence comes on the crowd. Keep in mind that these people are Hindus who have never heard of Jesus, yet some see Him with a crown of thorns; others beheld Him with the crown of a king; while some saw a pillar of fire in the midst of our tent. They've never read a Bible or heard about the Lord, but as they describe what they saw, it lines up with scripture!

"Once the glory manifests, the miracles begin, and they continue to build as we let the people share their own testimonies, giving glory to Jesus for what He's just done in their lives.

"We were humbled by what we saw—the sheer beauty of His presence—and what His love does for the people: The blind saw, the deaf heard, cripples danced for joy, the paralyzed received use of their limbs again, cancers were dissolved, and people on their death beds were healed! Every night testimonies came forth of instant healings after people saw angels, flashes of light, felt power similar to electric currents, or felt an invisible hand touch them.

"Many times I find it difficult to express in words the power, compassion, and mercy of Jesus Christ. Thousands of people came into the kingdom after hearing the Gospel and after witnessing the glory of God. It seemed to us that everyone who attended the meetings made Jesus their Lord and Savior."

Once these people see God's power and glory in manifestation, the news spreads like wildfire. The crowds grow in size night after night, and multitudes gladly make Jesus their Lord and Savior. The manifestation of the glory of God is for the expansion of the kingdom of God!

MUSLIM NATIONS SEE HIS GLORY

Aren't we all going to be surprised when the next great awakening is amongst the Muslims? (AB, 1988)

My good friend and fellow Coloradan, Jim Rogers, has been blessed with favor to preach the gospel around the world, including in many Muslim nations. Since Jesus the Healer is mentioned throughout the Koran, they give him permission to preach healing and minister to the sick. Here are some of his experiences with the glory of God over the last few years, starting with an experience in Cuba:

> **GOLD-DUST HEALING:** "I have been blessed to see the glory of God in several manifestations. Sometimes it comes as a cloud that you can see through; at other times, it's so thick that you can't see through it at all. Once when we were in a worship service in Cuba, I felt the Lord say to wash the Cuban leaders' feet. So as we washed their feet, what appeared to be little gold dust particles fell to the ground and upon the people. The presence of God became very, very thick and people started getting healed with no one touching them or praying for them. Knees, backs, deaf ears, and one man's blind eyes were healed."

Jim Rogers explains: "One thing that seems to invite this level of the presence is high praise and pure worship, but it can also happen during the message or during the time of ministry to people. It manifests sometimes over the platform—just all of a sudden the haze appears. There are times when you are preaching, and it forms around you and almost obscures you. There are other times when I look out over the crowd, and it forms over the entire group."

Here are some of Jim's experiences of the glory in some of the Muslim countries of the world:

LEPERS HEALED: "Some of the most dramatic times when the glory manifests are when it can be seen as a visible, tangible cloud. One night we were holding a crusade in a stadium. As we praised the Lord, we saw what looked like a physical cloud coming into the stadium. It was about 35 feet across and 20 feet in diameter. We knew that this was the glory of God. This night a group of about 45 lepers were together, and none of the crowd wanted to get near them. The glory cloud descended and came down right on the lepers. It literally enveloped them—we couldn't see them for about fifteen minutes! We continued to praise Jesus, but everyone in the stadium was looking at the cloud. When it lifted off of them and ascended, every one of those former untouchables was completely healed—nothing missing and everything restored!

What happened next blessed me the most. When the crowd saw what the Lord had done for these 45 people, they rushed around them and started hugging, embracing and expressing their love to them!"

DEAD RAISED: "I was at a house meeting for pastors, and we were discussing keys on how to continue in a move of God that was happening in this country. Suddenly there was a knock on the door. Keep in mind, we were in a dangerous country and had kept our meeting place a secret. We opened the door, and here was a man holding his 8-year-old daughter's body in his arms. He was holding a piece of paper with our address on it, and he said the Holy Spirit spoke it to him and told him to bring her here for prayer. His daughter had died four days earlier in the village where they lived, and he had carried her body for four days to get to this address! The smell coming from her body was horrible, and she had taken on a dark grey color.

"We laid her on a large coffee table in the main room of the house, and I told the pastors to all pray at once over this girl. As we prayed, the presence of God became so thick that several of the pastors could not stand and dropped to their knees. You could see the room fill up with what looked like haze. All of a sudden the little girl's eyes fluttered, and she sat up! In the time it took her to sit up, God restored her skin, and she was completely fine.

"We all praised God for about 20 minutes, and then there was another knock on the door. When we opened the door, another man and his friend were carrying his dead teenage son on a stretcher. He was holding a piece of paper as well—the Lord had also given him our address! His son was lying there in his underwear and had been shot in the chest three days earlier. This time the national pastors were very confident and told this father to lay his son on the coffee table. We gathered around him, started to pray, and the presence became very thick again with haze filling the room. All of a sudden the teenager's body began to bounce up and down on the table! I seriously thought that the table was going to shatter. As we watched his body bounce, all of a sudden his eyes opened. God had brought life back into his body. The father had brought with him a pair of pants and a shirt for his son to wear home—faith!"

These things will come to pass in the last days. God will display His glory. **(AB)**

IS ALL THIS IMPORTANT TO GOD?

Notice what God decreed as He spoke to Moses: "But truly, as I live, all the earth shall be filled with the glory of the Lord" (Numbers 14:21). Does God live? Well this is a vow He has made to show how serious He is about this! And just like it happened with Moses, the more we experience God, the more we get to know Him and the greater He becomes to us. Let's face it, experiencing God is kind of like the old potato chip commercial that said, "I bet you can't eat just one!"

"The glory of the Lord shall be revealed, and all flesh shall see it together; for the mouth of the Lord has spoken" (Isaiah 40:5). That's clearly what He's after—His glory being seen! Notice, all flesh, every person, will get a chance to see Him as He really is. "For the earth will be filled with the knowledge of the glory of the Lord, as the waters cover the sea" (Habakkuk 2:14).

> *I truly believe all the earth shall see the glory of the Lord! Not everyone will receive Him, but all men will be without excuse who reject Him in that unmistakable day of His visitation. It is coming!* **(AB)**

> *I believe the time has come when we must allow God to manifest Himself, moving in and through us. Then we will be effective ministers,*

demonstrating the presence and power of God.
(AB)

WHAT SHOULD IT MEAN TO US?

How much do we value the Presence and the glory of God? Will we be a people who desire it? Will we be a people who believe for it? Above all else, will we be a people who steward it to the honor and glory of His great Name? If we will sincerely ask Him, He will bring us to the point where the glory of God means to us what it means to Him. God's glory is to be the center of all things. The worship, attention, focus, and fame are all His!

"Be exalted, O God, above the heavens; let Your glory be above all the earth" (Psalm 57:5).

CHAPTER 11
NOW IS THE TIME

"It shall come as a breath ... and the breath shall
bring the wind ... and the wind shall bring the rain.
And there shall be floods and floods and floods ...
and torrents and torrents and torrents. Souls shall
be saved like falling leaves from mighty oaks swept
by a hurricane. Arms and legs will come down
from heaven ... and there shall be no ebb."

–1936 Prophecy

ARTHUR RECEIVED THIS prophecy when he was
24 years old. He says that out of all the prophecies he has heard over the years, this is the only one he has ever remembered word for word. It's as if this was burned into his memory by a branding iron! Two years ago, when he was 99, he said that we are on the brink of its beginning. Once it starts, there will be no ebb; in other words, it will not stop, recede, or let up.

> *When a tide comes in, it reaches high tide and then*
> *after flowing in, it ebbs out. Every move of God*
> *has been followed by the ebb. There is something*
> *lying ahead that will have no ebb!* **(AB)**

WIGGLESWORTH PROPHECY

Smith Wigglesworth prophesied in 1947 that there would come a time when churches that emphasized the Word would come together with churches that emphasized the Spirit. When these two come together, it will be the biggest move of God that the nations have ever seen. It will mark the beginning of a revival that will eclipse anything that has ever come upon the earth. "And there shall be no ebb."

In 2012 Jim Rogers was ministering in an African Muslim nation and was permitted to hold an open air meeting. As they worshiped the Lord on the platform, a native pastor whose hand had been amputated as a result of persecution suddenly had a completely new hand grow back! The last thing they watched grow back was his fingernails. Everyone present looked on in amazement! After this took place, 150 amputees missing hands, legs, arms, and feet lined up in front of the platform. Then a wave of miracle healing power swept from one end of the line to the other, and each person's missing limbs were restored! I asked Jim how long it took for each person to have his or her limb restored and he said, "About five seconds each. I saw it up close and it blew my mind. At first, I could hardly take it in!"

People of all nations, backgrounds, and religions are coming to the Lord *en masse* as they behold the power and glory of the Living Christ. They are discovering that

Jesus is more than a healer and a great teacher—He is the Lord and Savior of all humanity! "Souls shall be saved like falling leaves from mighty oaks swept by a hurricane. Arms and legs will come down from heaven."

An army of ordinary people
A kingdom where love is the key
A city, a light to the nations
Heirs to the promise are we
A people whose life is in Jesus
A nation together we stand
Only through grace are we worthy
Inheritors of the land

A people without recognition
But with Him a destiny sealed
Called to a heavenly vision
His purpose shall be fulfilled
Come, let us stand strong together
Abandon ourselves to the King
His love shall be ours forever
This victory song we shall sing

Chorus
A new day is dawning
A new age to come
When the children of promise
Shall flow together as one

A truth long neglected
But the time has now come
When the children of promise
Shall flow together as one.[1]

I am convinced about this: We are standing on the threshold of the last move of God which is going to be in the demonstration and might of His Holy Spirit. We are on the brink. It's now! **(AB)**

The prophet Isaiah tells us of a time when thick darkness, deep gloom, and depression shall cover the nations of the earth, but upon us the Lord shall shine, and over us His glory shall appear (see Isaiah 60:2). Now is the time for us to break out of our boxes, flow with the Spirit, and see King Jesus cover the earth with His glory! As I close out this book, I appeal to you with all of my heart to allow nothing to hold you back. We are coming into His finest that He's purposed for us all along. Now is the time!

ENDNOTES

Chapter 2: The Glory of God?
1. Jesus Culture Band, featuring Kim Walker-Smith, Chris Quilala, "Show Me Your Glory," from the album *My Passion – EP*, copyright © 2010 by Jesus Culture Music.

Chapter 3: Yours Is the Glory Forever!
1. Albert Hibbert, *Smith Wigglesworth: The Secret of His Power*, copyright © 1982 by Albert Hibbert (Tulsa, OK: Harrison House, Inc., 1982), pp. 14-16.

Chapter 4: How Have the Mighty Fallen?
1. "Statistics on Pastors," Dr. Richard J. Krejcir, Francis A. Schaeffer Institute of Church Leadership Development, copyright © 2007 (research from 1989 to 2006) by R. J. Krejcir, Ph.D.; http://www.intothyword.org/apps/articles/?articleid=36562.

Chapter 5: Catching the Spider
1. Andrew Murray, *Humility* (Springfield, PA: Whitaker House, 1982), pp. 10, 97.
2. C.S. Lewis, *Mere Christianity*, copyright © 1952 (renewed © 1980) by C.S. Lewis Pte. Ltd. (HarperSanFrancisco, a division of HarperCollinsPublishers, New York, 2000), p. 122.

3. J. Oswald Sanders, *Spiritual Maturity: Principles of Spiritual Growth for Every Believer*, copyright © 1962, 1994 by the Moody Bible Institute of Chicago (Chicago, IL: Moody Publishers, 1994), p. 62.

4. *On Lying in Bed and Other Essays by G.K. Chesterton,* edited by Alberto Manguel (Calgary, Alberta, Canada: Bayeux Arts, 2000), p. 508.

5. *New Bible Dictionary,* 3rd ed., edited by I. Howard Marshall, J.I. Packer, D.J. Wiseman, A.R. Millard (Downers Grove, IL: InterVarsity Press, 1996).

6. Gary Stephens, sermon, "How to Recognize the Snare of Pride," edited and posted by Cheryl Toepfer, December 28, 2012, http://accomplishthepurpose.blogspot.com/2012/12/the-snare-of-pride.html.

7. A.W. Tozer, *The Pursuit of God*, Tozer Legacy Edition (Camp Hill, PA: Christian Publications, Inc., 1982), p. 112.

Chapter 6: The Domino Club
1. Gordon Lindsay, *John Alexander Dowie* (Dallas, TX: Christ for the Nations, Inc., 1980), p. 140.

2. Ibid., pp. 140-143.

Chapter 7: To Judge or Not to Judge
1. Valerie Cox, "The Cookie Thief," posted by Sara Washburn, September 1, 2008, http://

sarawashburn.com/post/669455/the-cookie-thief-humanity-and-humility. Thank you, and bless you for sharing this with all the rest of us!

Chapter 8: A Beautiful Heart
1. Misty Edwards, "Beautiful Heart," copyright © 2009 Misty Edwards/Forerunner Music (ASCAP), 3535 E. Red Bridge Rd., Kansas City, MO 64137.

Chapter 9: Originations Are All Important
1. Smith Wigglesworth, *Ever Increasing Faith*, Revised Edition (Springfield, Missouri: Gospel Publishing House, 1971) , p. 118.
2. Ibid., p. 97.
3. Ibid., p. 142.

Chapter 11: Now Is the Time
1. Dave Bilbrough, "An Army of Ordinary People," copyright © 1983, Thankyou Music (admin. by EMI Christian Music Publishing). All rights reserved. International copyright secured.

ABOUT THE AUTHOR

Steve C. Shank is founder and senior pastor of City on the Hill Church in Boulder, Colorado, where he has served for 35 years. He is also founder of Confirming the Word Bible College in Boulder, now in its fourth year.

He has traveled extensively around the world, having made 80 mission trips at the time of this writing. You can hear him daily on his radio program, "The God-Kind of Life," on Denver's KLTT radio station.

If you would like to hear messages from Steve or purchase his other book, *Schizophrenic God? Finding Reality in Conflict, Confusion, and Contradiction*, go to his website at www.stevecshank.com or visit Amazon.com to order in paperback or e-book.

To contact Steve C. Shank or to arrange for him to come to your church group, conference, or Bible school, please write, e-mail, or call:

7483 Arapahoe Rd.
Boulder, CO 80303-1511
303-440-3873 (Office)
www.stevecshank.com

STEVE C. SHANK

Photo Courtesy of Haven Shank

18879218R00117

Made in the USA
San Bernardino, CA
03 February 2015